UNREFINED
FIND YOUR PURPOSE

By

Artem Gonchakov

For those who seek absolute freedom

CONTENTS

AFTERTHOUGHTS 182

APPENDIX A. PERSONAL MATURITY FRAMEWORK . .185

ABOUT THE AUTHOR 196

REFERENCES 198

SECTION I - AWARENESS

When I reflect on my personal story and how things have turned out, I find it amusing that life has always provided me with opportunities to create something special.

I've used those chances to go from being a clueless kid in a small Ukrainian city to building a successful career in the United States, working on Wall Street, living in Manhattan, making billions for my clients, running global initiatives alongside influential people, starting my own business, becoming a CEO, earning my first million, buying a few houses, and traveling the globe.

What you ultimately choose to do might not feel unique to other people, but for you, it definitely will. And the bigger the struggle, the more rewarding the outcome. The moment you recognize and appreciate this, your personal journey will become far richer and more meaningful.

This book is my attempt to make a small difference in the world. I've documented my own turning points and sprinkled in stories of famous people for reflection. I love creating systems for almost everything, and most people appreciate concrete steps to reach their goals, so this should be a win–win. The world is an endless source of learning, and I'm fascinated by the kind of knowledge that truly guides us. I want to share it all with you, so you can transition into a more meaningful existence.

Up to the age of seventeen, nothing in my life felt special. I went to a normal kindergarten and struggled through public school like everyone else. Homework was a burden, and I was always looking for ways to avoid it. Once, I challenged my history teacher to a video game match for a grade because I thought it would save me from a month of studying. He agreed, but little did I know that he was an expert at that specific strategy game, called Cossacks: European Wars. His deep knowledge of history was practically a cheat code. My miscalculation cost me more work and extra assignments in the end. Surprisingly, he liked me because no one had ever challenged him like that before. He later became my history professor at university, which made my life easier there.

I had no friends until the eighth grade, so I overcompensated for my lack of personal connections by poking fun at others. Any opportunity to make a silly comment felt good, as if I were announcing to the world that I existed. I also looked for ways to show resistance to any form of systemic control at school - no matter how small or big. When my school introduced a uniform with specific designs and colors, I convinced my parents to create a different style just for me.

Eventually, my father was called to the principal's office because I was breaking the dress code. He told the principal that he was colorblind (not true) and we couldn't afford a new uniform (true). He somehow persuaded the principal to let me keep wearing it. I still don't know why my parents agreed to all this, but it gave me a thrill. I was clearly showing off, yet I was never a "cool kid," more like a great pretender who wanted to stand out. Unsurprisingly, most teachers didn't like me, and my father's face would turn red at every parent–teacher meeting when new stories came out. Still, he rarely gave me trouble over it; maybe he sensed something I didn't. Occasionally, he would say, "Son, do whatever you want with your life, but never harm people." I used to find that funny, never realizing how powerful that message was - or how it quietly reinforced the idea that I could do things my own way, even if others didn't agree.

At home, no big events ever happened, and I spent most of my time alone watching TV. American shows, movies, and cartoons kept me occupied. I played soccer for a local team but never excelled and eventually quit, without forming any friendships. Later in life I realized that being on the field, playing the game made me free and it was something I truly enjoyed. Till this day I think quitting was one of my biggest mistakes in life. I often felt bored and never knew how to make the best use of my time. I wasn't asking myself existential questions back then, but I had a constant feeling that something wasn't right - that there must be more to life than this.

My parents were busy trying to make a living in post-Soviet Ukraine during the 1990s, so they couldn't pay much attention to my struggles - not out of ignorance but necessity. They were focused on survival. Thanks to them, another big lesson fell into my lap without me realizing it - you have to figure out how to make it despite the circumstances. Jobs, medicine, and food were all scarce. If you didn't find a way to get supplies, you went hungry. My father once grilled meat at a local kebab stall, and my mother sold fish in the freezing Ukrainian winter just to keep us afloat.

I remember one night when I had a crazy fever. The ambulance came but had no medicine, which was typical. My father ran around in the middle of the night knocking on neighbors' doors for help. A nurse next door offered something from her own emergency stash. There were no clean needles; it was all makeshift. But for me, this was normal. I didn't know any better. Yet, thanks to TV, I knew there was a different world out there - I just had to find a way to reach it.

My parents trusted me to figure things out and only checked my grades once a year. Our sole agreement was that I would pass everything required to move on to the next stage of school. How I made it happen was up to me. This turned out to be one of the greatest gifts they ever gave me - the ability to find my own way through difficult situations. Over time, I mastered that skill.

Looking back, aside from school, I spent most of my time alone, lacking the basic social knowledge and experiences that teach you how life should or shouldn't be. I didn't know how to behave in different situations and felt especially awkward one-on-one. I never knew what to say. I always felt a few steps behind, like I was twenty-eight with the mindset of an eighteen-year-old. That gap left me feeling "not smart enough" or "not worthy," which planted seeds of insecurity that I had to fight later on. On the other hand, it forced me to rely on myself and do whatever it took to move forward. Gradually, I began to trust that I could change my life if I truly wanted to.

I often felt torn between two extremes: following a traditional path with predictable outcomes - strongly influenced by family and society - or venturing into the unknown, breaking rules and finding my own way to impact the world. I wasn't mentally strong enough to fully commit to the latter, so I ended up on the more conventional route. Yet I never let go of the idea of greatness, the belief that "magic" was possible. It showed up in different ways throughout my so-called "ordinary" life: finishing school, then university, landing a serious job, climbing the corporate ladder, and starting a family. In many ways, it was the American Dream.

But the journey was tough, and I don't want to minimize that. It also turned out that I never truly cared about my professional achievements. Checking off each "success" felt like following a script someone else had written. Whenever I reached a big milestone, like closing a multi-million-dollar deal for my company in record breaking time or saving over a billion dollars for Elon Musk to rescue a company from bankruptcy, I'd share it with friends and family. They'd be excited, but my own reaction was usually a shrug - "Yeah, whatever." I'd feel good for a moment then slip back into numbness, sensing that it still wasn't enough. I sometimes fantasized about walking out of my apartment and just vanishing. I think people saw me as ungrateful, and maybe I was. Each accomplishment gave me only a brief high before plunging me back into the same old feeling - a widening gap between what I wanted and what I got.

Clinging to a traditional life while hungering for a deeper purpose led me to explore psychology, philosophy, self-help, personal development, and various ideologies to find a more meaningful existence. Changing my core beliefs about something important turned out to be much harder than landing the next promotion. Some changes took me years - maybe because that's how long it takes, or maybe because I was navigating it all alone, paying the price for feeling disconnected for so long. I realized every struggle boiled down to one root cause: fear. Due to my fear of losing something (acceptance, stability, status), I let others influence me into fitting a system, even when it felt wrong. While parts of my life turned out well, others went south, including my early divorce.

I was stuck in a normal life I didn't really enjoy, waiting for "something special" to happen - naïve, in hindsight. The truth is, a special life doesn't come with instructions, while a traditional one has a clear blueprint of what success "should" look like. That's probably why so few people take the extraordinary route.

My Transformation started when I was seventeen and I found books by Valerii Sinelnikov on the power of the subconscious mind. I didn't understand much about what he had to say then, but it consumed me. He taught me that what I felt was a manifestation of my potential - that life would keep giving me opportunities to reach a better state. My mind, if harnessed well, would remind me of everything I dreamed of achieving. It was the first step on a very long hero's journey of self-discovery. All I knew at that point was that I had to be ready to recognize and accept whatever opportunities came my way.

It's no surprise that people of all ages and backgrounds struggle to find their Life Purpose - it's a widespread phenomenon. A study from the Cultural Research Center at Arizona Christian University suggests 75% of millennials are desperately seeking meaning and purpose in their lives. Another study from Nashville-based Lifeway Research shows that COVID 19 shifted many Americans' perspectives: 1 in 5 think about their Life Purpose every single day, and 57% are searching for more meaning overall. Yet another study found a correlation between a sense of purpose and a decreased mortality rate. In other words, lacking a clear purpose leads to emotional and physical stress. Without a reason to push through life's difficulties, it's easy to give up or adopt unhealthy coping mechanisms. Mine were video games and alcohol. A purposeless life can feel unbearable, leading to a hollow existence and leaving you vulnerable to others' influence. That, in turn, fosters emotional imbalance, health issues, and a craving for quick fixes.

This book catalogs the journey I've taken to reach a better state of mind. I've gathered and structured the knowledge and wisdom I've gained from my successes and failures. I wish someone had guided me more so I wouldn't have had to stumble alone so often. That's why I'm excited to share all this with you. If you're reading these pages, that means I've finally found my purpose - and I want to show you how you can find yours, too. At the very least, I hope my experiences, both good and bad, will ignite a spark that encourages you to create the life you truly want.

It's normal to crave meaningful events, powerful emotions, and extraordinary experiences. We're all capable of making a difference - no matter how small - and creating a story that could inspire others and leave us with no regrets. True greatness comes from the journey toward your Personal Maturity - the process of becoming the real you, capable of living up to your true potential. I'll use this term formally throughout the book because I wanted a single concept to hold all my ideas about searching for purpose. Personal Maturity has become the foundation of all the Transformations I'll share with you.

Personal Maturity is a set of beliefs, patterns, processes, principles, frameworks, and guides to give you the confidence and practical know-how to craft the life you've always wanted. It's something I've repeatedly applied to my own life, sometimes without realizing it. Through moments of pain and joy, I eventually shaped a system that feels almost too simple - but it should feel that way. My goal is to show you that finding your purpose doesn't have to be monumental and that you can begin at any stage of your life.

Creating awareness is the first, critical step in designing your life. We all have the capacity for greatness; we just need to unlock it. Personal Maturity can become your unique ideology because it offers the missing components, common sense, and logical steps needed to build the life you want. Ultimately, though, it has to be personal to you.

Here's how this book is structured:

- Section 1: Creating awareness. You'll learn about the challenges that keep you from finding your purpose.

- Section 2: Designing your life. You'll discover how to establish a foundation, build structure, and understand Life fundamental elements.

- Section 3: Developing a Growth Mindset. You'll learn how Personal Maturity fits into the bigger picture.

- Section 4: Becoming effective and efficient. You'll learn best practices for overcoming the challenges from Section 1, while leveling up by applying the principles from Sections 2 and 3.

I encourage you to practice everything in this book. Apply critical thinking and bring your creativity along for the ride.

Let's begin by understanding why finding purpose is both so difficult and so important.

CHAPTER I

LOST LIFE PURPOSE

> *"When a man can't find a deep sense of meaning, they distract themselves with pleasure"*
>
> — **Viktor Frankl**

The biggest life Transformation happens when you hit rock bottom. When there's nothing to lose, ironically, you feel free - you're finally in charge. Most of the time, we're terrified of failing, so we float in the middle of nowhere, without a clear direction. Those who learn to let go can have everything.

There was a woman who couldn't find a stable career after graduating from university. She lost her mother to multiple sclerosis, her marriage failed, and she had to move to another country with her infant daughter. With no job, she survived on welfare benefits, barely making ends meet. Yet despite the hardships, she found solace in writing. It helped her cope with her struggles, and eventually, she finished her first manuscript. After being rejected by at least twelve publishers, Bloomsbury finally accepted her work. This is how Harry Potter and the Philosopher's Stone came into existence, and how J.K. Rowling became one of the most successful authors in history.

Rediscovering a sense of purpose under such circumstances can feel hopeless. J.K. Rowling could have given up many times, but she persisted, finding meaning despite hardship. Many people don't even try, convinced that success in the face of huge challenges is impossible - this belief often becomes a self-fulfilling prophecy.

Although the concept of purpose has philosophical roots, it can also be surprisingly controversial. Today, we focus more on rewards than on value, often driven by a consumption mindset. A reward is a short-term benefit - nothing wrong with that, in theory. But if it's your main feedback mechanism, it can corrupt your motivation by promoting greed. I used to chase promotions day and night, driven by pure greed. I made terrible decisions, racked up health issues, and ruined relationships - just to maintain a job title. Growing up in the bleak reality of 1990s Ukraine made me prioritize fast results and become self-centered, without stopping to think critically. I needed rewards to feel both progress and safety. Sure, this mindset works well for building financial wealth, which is why so many people are obsessed with money. But I've learned that greed can't feed purpose - it's usually a sign that you don't have one. You need value - a long-term benefit mechanism - and you have to be willing to sacrifice some rewards to get it.

J.K. Rowling created huge value by writing Harry Potter, building an entire movement around it. Imagine if she had just rushed through the book to make some quick cash and escape her financial struggles. The story might have turned out very differently, and I'm glad we'll never know. You don't need a Life Purpose to create value, but one can lead to the other.

I've identified three reasons why people struggle to find their purpose, and we will explore each of these reasons in detail in the following chapters:

- Follower's Mindset: We're usually raised to be followers rather than leaders or creators.

- Borrowed Success: We don't learn how to build our own success, so we end up repeating someone else's.

- Social Debt: We're forced to meet other people's high expectations and rarely consider our own needs, generating and accumulating social guilt.

You may be dealing with at least one of these challenges - maybe all three. Even one can trigger self-doubt, daily stress, and deep internal conflict, often leading to a mental breaking point. The result? You blend into society, stand in line like everybody else, and accept the harsh reality of mediocrity. Very few escape unscathed.

J.K. Rowling broke free from all three challenges after hitting rock bottom, proving her dedication to a sense of purpose - a Transformation most people only dream of. Hers is just another example of the hero's journey.

In her 2008 Harvard commencement address, she said, "Failure meant a stripping away of the inessential. I stopped pretending to myself that I was anything other than what I was, and began to direct all my energy into finishing the only work that mattered to me. Had I really succeeded at anything else, I might never have found the determination to succeed in the one arena where I truly belonged."

These challenges are a social construct, designed to accommodate five key elements. I call it "Life in the Nutshell" (Figure 1) because at a glance, an average life is highly predictable and leaves little room for greatness. We have a Job, which only few people can turn into a truly successful career; a Hobby that might become a job, if you are lucky enough; a Family comprised of your relationship with your parents, partner, and children; Friendship, which ideally is long-lasting and meaningful; and an Ideology, which is a socially constructed way to understand and navigate the world.

Life in the Nutshell

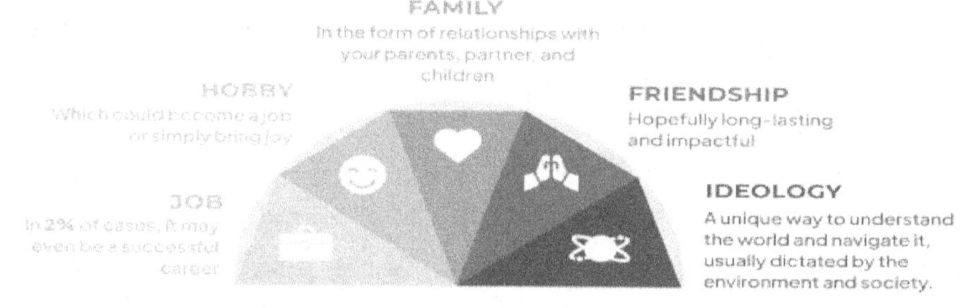

Figure 1. "Life in the Nutshell"

That's basically it - nothing more, nothing less. Anyone who lives "Life in the Nutshell" without a clear purpose will be consumed by these elements, struggling to find meaning in any of them. Society gives us these five elements so we can "contribute," yet we often end up trapped, living within a framework someone else defined with little decision-making power. Rarely does anyone ask or help you to figure out what you truly want. On the other hand, if you dare to Dream big and chase ambitious goals, you'll have less time for these five elements and end up being judged by a society that expects you to be a "good citizen" - live by the book, never break rules, never want more or something special - conform. Maybe you'll try to balance both and get stuck in limbo - like I did - never really excelling at anything. Mediocrity. Worst state to be in. I secretly wished to hit rock bottom so I could start transforming my life, yet I was too afraid to change anything. I felt like I had to justify my existence to the world.

To understand why "Life in the Nutshell" is so powerful at keeping you under control, we need to go back to childhood.

From an early age, you're introduced to each of the five elements, step by step. First, you exist and behave around your parents and immediate relatives, absorbing whatever traditions and ideologies they follow. Of course, you don't have the cognitive ability to question any of it. You don't even know what "ideology" means, so you just go along with it. My parents used to say, "Don't question us; we're the authority." I had no idea how deeply that would affect me later. For instance, at work I felt a huge fear of my managers. I couldn't talk to them without feeling like I had to avoid conflict at all costs, so I'd just do whatever they asked. One time, I waited four hours - until 2 a.m. - for my managers to answer just two questions, which only took ten minutes of their time. I never asked to schedule a better time; I just went along. It took me years to fix that mindset.

After you learn how family dynamics work, you move into your first layer of society: kindergarten and school. You might develop friendships, each with its own social system. The more time you spend together, the more you're exposed to their rules and beliefs, which shape your own responses. You start comparing yourself to others, like when kids say, "I want that toy because my friend has it." That constant comparison follows you into adulthood, creating a false sense of needing things you never wanted in the first place. Adults do the same, following celebrities to copy their looks, outfits, or lifestyles. Add peer pressure to the mix, and you have a recipe for mental decline.

That's how I started drinking. Once I joined a social group that revolved around drinking until we couldn't stand up. Getting wasted helped me fit in with my "friends." I'd do dumb stuff just for them to like me. I once mixed beer, wine, vodka, and who knows what else just to prove myself, and I ended up vomiting and blacking out. That kind of behavior became my way of being the center of attention and fitting in. Later, drinking became a coping mechanism for stress and negative emotions - my go-to solution.

Eventually, you reach the final stage of the social order. After university, you land your first job, and now you're a fully functioning, obedient member of society. You pick up political rhetoric, learn to pay taxes, and complain about life like a "proper" adult. I studied Computer Science simply because someone in my school, whom I thought was smart, chose it. So I dove into five years of madness without blinking. By the final year, a classmate mentioned an interview with some company, so I went too - no extra thought required. I got the job without fully understanding what it was or why I wanted it. My parents were ecstatic: I'd checked all the boxes - finished school, went to university, got a job. Nobody asked what I really wanted, and I was too scared to disappoint anyone, so I stuck to the traditional path. Inside, I felt resistance but didn't have enough mental power to name it. This tension showed up as small acts of rebellion - like back in school where I was a "scared troublemaker." I did just enough to feel like I was making my own decisions, but not enough to get fired or be disliked. I was a decade behind on my Personal Maturity journey.

And so it goes. You shuffle through family, friends, school, university, and maybe a hobby or two until you end up in a job you never wanted. If you're lucky, you start a family as well. By the time you're old enough to make your own decisions, you've been indoctrinated into an ideology you're not supposed to question. People don't like those who stand out, so you pass the same mindset down to your kids.

Your "success" in life gets defined by how you split your time among these five elements - spending too much time at a job you hate, too little on a hobby you love, ignoring friendships, or pouring too much energy into a family dynamic that stresses you out. Society assigns you a label based on your contributions and progress in each element, which can make it hard to forge your own path.

Whatever your situation, you might end up chasing the wrong career, escaping reality, seeking constant validation from friends and family, or following false ideologies. For years, I believed that "making it" in life was all about following along and not causing trouble. Whenever I stepped out of line, I felt guilty - like I'd broken some sacred rule and deserved punishment. That turned me into a perfectionist with unrealistic expectations. I wanted to get everything right on the first try, and if I didn't, I felt worthless. Sometimes I'd keep pushing on something I shouldn't have pursued, just to prove I could do it perfectly. This also made me a terrible leader, because I never trusted anyone else to do any important tasks - I thought only I could do them better. And yet I often gave up on things too soon; I'd be inches from a breakthrough and just quit, feeling awful afterward, blaming myself for not being "good enough."

My parents also told me to never stand out. I'd listen, but what I saw on TV was different. Cool stuff happened to people who didn't conform. "Life in the Nutshell" consumes you, keeps you busy forever, and leaves no space for greatness. There's no energy to resist, and you can't see any other way of living, so you're ready to give up. That's why existential questions often get labeled as "just philosophical" - there's no time for them when you're barely surviving under social pressure.

Eventually, something cracks because you can't maintain this forever. The gap between your job, family, friends, hobbies, and ideology grows, leaving you emptier by the day. You have to choose: you can either fight for balance in "Life in the Nutshell" or step outside it to chase something other people might not understand or support. If you don't make that choice, you might drift toward depression, illness, and addictions, and then surrender to mediocrity. Nobody taught you how to define your purpose or gave you any guidance on how to do it. We rely on our parents, but they often don't know much either. This has never been an individual problem - it's a systemic one. You're left to solve it alone. Deep down, you're scared of how your story ends, knowing that life can be depressingly predictable.

I don't know anyone who's successfully nailed all five elements of "Life in the Nutshell." There's always something - a traumatic childhood, loneliness, poor education, a toxic job, an overinflated ego, or narcissism. Personally, I often took the easy way out with artificial substitutes like gaming and drinking, so I could escape reality for a while and leave tomorrow's problems for tomorrow. Ignorance becomes an odd comfort zone, promoted worldwide by public channels and influencers who tell us how to live. The more you rely on artificial consumption instead of a dedicating yourself meaningful life, the heavier your regret will be when you're older. It eats away at your soul. People crave purpose, sometimes without even knowing it.

Let me ask, which is worse: Slowly nearing the end of your life riddled with regrets but doing nothing to change, or failing while you fight for something great?

Why Does It Matter?

We all have that strange feeling inside - at least occasionally - that we're capable of something more. It's why you feel awesome when you create anything. Deep down, we know we're built for greatness, but we've been taught to choose comfort and to fear that part of ourselves.

People do dream big. You have the courage to take small actions, at least enough to say, "I lived the life I wanted."

We're both scared and fascinated by the unknown. We're curious creatures, hungry to learn what's next, sometimes for our own sake, sometimes for the greater good. As a child, you were curious about everything, but then someone told or forced you to think, act, or do things their way. They believed they were right, and it suppressed your uniqueness under social expectations.

What's the alternative if you ignore your purpose? A delusional utopia curated by "the wisdom of the crowd" for the unwise. That will create a massive void of unfulfilled potential that can turn destructive. In moments of silence, it will haunt you. Simply put, you'll regret it.

So does having a family, a job, hobbies, friends, and an ideology mean you can't have a purposeful life? Of course not. I want you to make conscious decisions, apply critical thinking, and shape a life that's really yours. Maybe your Life Purpose is to excel in "Life in the Nutshell." But I want you to picture a mindset where you need no external motivation - everything just flows naturally, manifesting something the world has never seen.

Finding Your Purpose

Sometimes you see people so obsessed with an idea - odd or impossible at first - that they redefine what's "normal." They can't fit into "Life in the Nutshell," and society struggles to handle them without causing harm. These people are ready to sacrifice everything for a greater cause - a "necessary evil" that drives evolution.

When you think about it, most of what exists today came from people who imagined something bigger and better or simply disagreed with the status quo and dared to challenge generations of "established" wisdom. We need more people like that, and it should be inevitable.

What if we create a society that actually fosters innovation and encourages people to embark on a radical quest for purpose? People who start with "why" and genuinely find an answer. For that to happen society must be more tolerant of "mad geniuses" - people absolutely dedicated to their purpose and push the boundaries of what's normal.

We should keep improving the five core elements of "Life in a Nutshell," evolving social structures and our expectations to create a better foundation for those who want something beyond the norm. We need to reduce the numbness of artificial consumption. Less phoniness, more genuine engagement, so we don't drag the entire system down. No matter how grim things look, I believe humanity can continue pushing toward a more meaningful existence for anyone who wants it. In this book, I'll propose a logical path to help you take that first step.

Foundational Challenges

In the grand scheme of things, society places us in a box: "Life in the Nutshell." Our best option seems to be to obey, but when we don't, social pressure (and our own fears) can crush us. Over time, we learn to numb ourselves with distractions - and that's the Follower's Mindset. Some of us get really lost and end up copying someone else's path, hoping it'll solve our existential questions. That's Borrowed Success. If we ever try to break out of this box, guilt usually pulls us back. We're reminded of our obligations to everyone around us, so we abandon our wildest Dream - the "mad genius" inside us who wants to change the world. That's Social Debt. Each challenge forms part of a bigger puzzle, one that can trap you in a swirl of hopes, dreams, responsibilities, and demands - leaving no time to figure out what really matters. Ultimately, all of it can lead to a Lost Purpose.

That's a lot to deal with, so let's unpack it one by one. I'll break down each challenge in detail and then offer you a solution.

CHAPTER 2

FOLLOWER'S MINDSET

> *"To find yourself, think for yourself."*
>
> — Socrates

How many "gurus" do you follow? These days, countless people fall prey to fake influencers - social media snake-oil sellers who insist their way is the only way. Their reward is obvious. For you, it means drifting even further from your Personal Maturity journey. Most of these individuals abuse the "power" of having a massive following, convincing you to believe in their framework so they can get what they want, no matter the cost. Social media is just one avenue through which we can see the Follower's Mindset at work.

We follow coaches, gurus, business leaders, and prophets who promise a bright future and a great life. When done without critical thinking, it becomes a form of mental slavery. You end up bound to someone else's ideology - pushed to become an ideal replica of what a guru wants you to be. Confused and lost, you're ready to consume whatever is offered, tangled in the spider's web of comfortable but ultimately unfulfilling existence. All you wanted was an answer to your struggles, some relief from the chaos inside you. When someone claims to have all the answers, it's easier to follow their path than wander aimlessly with no direction. No questions asked.

I've been that person. I lacked maturity on so many levels and was ready to adopt any path presented to me. From the previous chapter, we know that misfits are often coerced to obey and punished if they don't - so I usually chose the safer option, staying in line. The system is designed this way, and I followed it for far too long.

Brian Epstein, best known as the manager of The Beatles, seemed to have it all: influence, wealth, and the admiration of millions. Yet behind the scenes, he struggled with his own identity and purpose, never really stepping out of the band's shadow. He wrestled with insecurities and social pressure while managing everything from their image to schedules, promotions, and contracts. In reality, he was building someone else's success story, blind to how it was damaging his soul. Brian lived vicariously through the band, never embracing his own potential outside their fame. His self-doubt and sense of inadequacy led to drug addiction and dangerous behavior. Ultimately, he couldn't confront these challenges, and his life ended tragically at the age of 32.

You might recognize this pattern already; I introduced it in the previous chapter. From childhood, you follow your parents' guidance until you develop enough courage to question things. Meanwhile, society tests your compliance. You start in kindergarten, move on to school, and then university, each time obeying rules and meeting standards to advance. If you don't, there's always punishment. It's the ultimate training ground for the major stages of life: job and family. You become an obedient unit of society, weighed down by responsibilities, daily stress, and a caffeine habit. You see it every day - sometimes we joke about it, trying to come to terms with our place in the ecosystem.

Deep down, I always sensed something was off, but like Brian, I found it safer to live according to someone else's guidance and stay confused. Because of my isolation earlier in life, I lagged behind socially; transferring decisions to others felt like a relief. Society said, "Get a stable job," so I did - even though all I really wanted was to play soccer. I figured that out too late, years after I'd quit to focus on the "normal" path. Society said, "Start a family," so I did. I got married at 25, clearly not ready, only to divorce six years later - realizing afterward how many mistakes could've been avoided. Society said, "Play along and don't question too much," so I did. I stayed paralyzed by fear, overthinking all the possible negative outcomes of big life decisions. In the end, most of my worries never materialized. That's the ultimate Follower's Mindset: follow along, wait for instructions, and do your best not to stand out.

Don't get me wrong - without rules and some level of control, society would collapse. We do need a fundamental structure to keep our evolutionary progress on track, hopefully prolonging humanity's survival. The real problem is that many adults never learn to think for themselves and fail to question what's happening around them. A lack of critical thinking creates the Follower's Mindset. As a result, these individuals can't build an environment that fosters a meaningful existence for themselves, let alone their children. On a bigger scale, this turns society toward consumption-driven behavior that's paraded as success.

I recall buying my first apartment purely to avoid "losing money" and feeling absolutely nothing afterward - yet people cheered and congratulated me on becoming a property owner. Every subsequent property I acquired felt similarly hollow. All the while, I was trying to figure out why I couldn't enjoy the fruits of my hard work. Eventually I realized that it was never my decision. I just went along with what everyone else said, never pausing to consider it for myself. Under social pressure, people would rather pay someone else to tell them what to do with their lives rather than make tough choices on their own. We forget who we really are and how to develop an authentic role in this rapidly evolving world.

It's a paradox. We're in an era of extraordinary technological progress, where new opportunities seem endless, yet this obedient style of living has bred confusion and existential crises. We've become an assembly line of consumption, crushing our innate ability to create, innovate, and stay curious. I remember times when I chose destructive consumption over personal Growth - scrolling social media for hours, blowing money on weekend shopping sprees, and ending up on the couch with video games and whiskey. I was sliding into a comfortable hole, losing my mental sharpness along the way.

Have you ever felt like comfort was killing your potential? I did - almost every night in bed, replaying my day, vowing to change everything tomorrow, only to repeat the same mistakes. Eventually, my body started giving out. I gained weight, developed two stomach ulcers, and had back issues. I even ended up in the ER, thinking I was having a heart attack. Over time, I grew terrified of dying and had regular panic attacks. I couldn't sleep in my own bed. Sometimes I'd sleep on the floor in another room or wander around at night, occasionally dozing off outdoors near my apartment complex.

This made me realize that I wasn't alone - mental health issues, such as depression, anxiety, and so much more, are surging like never before. They signal a deeper disconnect between the rapid pace of modern life, our well-being, and our path to Personal Maturity. We're stuck doing things we aren't meant to do. People spin in the vortex of social expectations as we chase promotions, save for a house, and try to meet moral standards and stay sane, all while an inner void grows, filled with missed opportunities and broken promises. Society should empower individuals to live their best possible lives, not turn them into blindsided followers with no Vision for a brighter future.

Steve Jobs is a prime example of someone who broke from the norm and revolutionized the tech industry by thinking differently. Early on, he struggled with direction - he dropped out of college, traveled to India in search of purpose, and was heavily influenced by mentors like Robert Friedland (who introduced him to the concept of the "reality distortion field") and Edwin Land (who showed how to merge art and science). Founding Apple and enjoying early success didn't stop him from getting fired in 1985 due to internal politics. Unwilling to conform, he founded NeXT and bought Pixar, continuing his quest for innovation and change. While he was gone, Apple nearly collapsed from a lack of innovation, weak leadership, and financial woes. They finally brought Jobs back in 1997, and with a renewed Vision, he refused to become a follower. Apple emerged as one of the most successful tech companies in the world. The rest is history.

Why aren't there more people like Steve? Perhaps because we scroll, shop, and consume our way through life, waiting and hoping for some spark to light us up rather than taking action and owning our destiny. We lose track of our potential. Sometimes we bury it to comply with social norms; other times, we're so lost we can't ignite it alone. With globalized social media - where likes, follows, and shares rule - it's easy to forget we can define our own unique purpose.

The Follower's Mindset is so woven into modern culture that it feels normal. There's always someone claiming they know exactly how you should live. They'll tell you what's right and wrong; to them, everything else is a false narrative. We start comparing ourselves to every new expert, pop culture icon, or internet sensation. We idolize them, forgetting they're only human, with flaws and insecurities of their own. Admiration itself isn't bad, but it becomes destructive when it morphs into blind imitation, smothering our built-in creativity.

Let's sum it up: for most of your life, you've been told what to do. Chances are, your attempts at carving a unique, purposeful path have been shut down by societal pressures and sky-high expectations. You've been pushed to follow and stay in line at every crucial juncture of your life. Your body and mind have occasionally signaled that there's a bigger opportunity out there, but you never pursued it. Now, you numb any pangs of guilt over your wasted potential through consumption. You're stuck in a role you hate or find unfulfilling and may have a growing risk of mental and physical health problems. It feels normal to be sad, depressed, and to question your very existence. You don't have time for yourself and end up picking the easiest route. That's life with the Follower's Mindset.

I will show you how to break from the Follower's Mindset, but first, it's time to look at what Borrowed Success is all about.

CHAPTER 3

BORROWED SUCCESS

> *"Do not go where the path may lead, go instead where there is no path and leave a trail."*
> — Ralph Waldo Emerson

Success is like a mirage.

You chase it desperately, striving for big wins, only to discover it's not what you expected. When success isn't connected to your journey toward Personal Maturity, it often strays from fulfillment, leaving you drained and dissatisfied - creating a false sense of accomplishment. Picture landing a long-desired promotion but feeling nothing. That's exactly how it was for me when I became Vice President of a fast-growing Wall Street startup. I spent eleven years working day and night, and all I felt was emptiness.

In my quest to understand why I reacted that way, I discovered two mental models for success: Borrowed Success and Life Success.

Borrowed Success is your ability to repeat success stories that have already been created and achieved by other people - often fueled by the Follower's Mindset. Society wants you to work through a well-defined list of "success stories" and will validate your efforts as long as you stay in line and perpetuate the illusion of a desirable life. That's because society needs control to avoid chaos. I borrowed a success story by chasing a promotion I thought would change my life. It didn't. I woke up the next day, went to work, and kept doing what I'd always done. The only real difference was that some people treated me differently - some with respect, others with fear or envy, depending on their own journeys.

Life Success is your ability to create something unique for the world, something that's never been done before. Ideas like this can be tough to accept and are often seen as the domain of geniuses. Ironically, as soon as you accomplish something truly new, you're enabling others to borrow that success. So is Borrowed Success necessarily bad? It's only problematic if your life is filled with hollow achievements you've borrowed - without ever using them as a stepping stone to create your own Life Success. A handful of people do leverage Borrowed Success to build something bigger, but most just keep chasing one borrowed goal after another, never aiming higher. As for me, I've begun my own quest to create Life Success, and this book is part of that journey.

Life Success is special - almost magical. How else would you describe that first time anyone accomplishes something previously deemed impossible? We celebrate the first person to summit Mt. Everest, the first to cure a once-untreatable disease, or the first to run a marathon under two hours. You likely know the name of the first person in space or the first to fly a plane - but probably not the second or third. People who come after that are essentially borrowing success. It's not necessarily bad; it's just how the Follower's Mindset reactivates itself once the "impossible" is proven possible.

Life Success happens when you embrace a Personal Maturity journey to accomplish something great - or "die" trying. This isn't about what you should do; it's about what you must do. It's the thing that ignites a fire in your soul, calling you toward a meaningful life. It could be on a grand scale or a humble one, but it's fundamentally yours. Life Success starts with a Dream or ambition, requires introspection, courage, and persistence, and involves taking risks and facing failures. Most of all, it means living in a way that's true to who you are - not who others want you to be. If you choose this path, life will hold you accountable and might just reward you with the greatest experience. If it feels right, you pursue it to the end, pushing boundaries, creating a new reality, and redefining what's possible. In the end, Life Success is about how you live, not just what you achieve.

Your Life Success doesn't have to be big; it just needs to be yours. For some, it might involve changing other people's lives. For others, it might be as simple as setting a world record in a video game. Willis Gibson, a 13-year-old from Oklahoma, did exactly that. On December 21, 2023 - after 40 years of people trying to "win" Tetris - he became the first to do it, earning hero status in the gaming community. In Tetris "winning" means breaking the game itself, and Willis figured out how, creating his first Life Success.

If cracking video games isn't your thing, you could go the opposite way, like Elon Musk did. Against all odds, he disrupted payment systems, space travel, and the auto industry. He's an example of someone who's created multiple Life Success stories and isn't stopping. I happened to work with Elon at Twitter on a few ambitious initiatives and can confirm that he pushes boundaries whenever he can, aiming for major global impact. He faced near-bankruptcy, repeated failures, and heavy criticism from the media and government. He's not here to borrow success; he's here to create a different future.

I spent years chasing Borrowed Success without even realizing there was another option - or how it would affect my mental health. Essentially, I lived someone else's life and constantly questioned my own. For instance, investing in real estate was easy because there are countless success stories and playbooks for it. I wasn't creating anything new; I was following an existing strategy for personal gain. It gave me zero satisfaction. Now that I understand the difference between Borrowed Success and Life Success, I use real estate as a safety net - one that frees my mind to focus on my Personal Maturity journey. It's not my ultimate goal; it's just a vehicle for something far more important. With no big expectations tied to it, I no longer need to obsess over its significance.

Don't chase Borrowed Success simply for the sake of it. There's a good chance you'll wake up one day confronted by regret in its darkest forms: loneliness, depression, addiction, anxiety, or all of the above. Eventually, you'll pay the highest price - wasting your life.

Because of our Follower's Mindset, many of us never find time or the will to craft a unique story, so we default to Borrowed Success. You've been judged at every stage of your life for both your achievements and the ones you missed. Sometimes people can't understand why you're not doing the obvious things - pursuing a certain career or chasing money as the main measure of success. But society's expectations were never about making you the "first" at anything; they're about creating a standardized social unit that won't break the status quo. It's easier to control.

That brings us to our next idea. Let's explore the concept of Social Debt.

CHAPTER 4

SOCIAL DEBT

> *"To be yourself in a world that is constantly trying to make you something else is the greatest accomplishment."*
>
> - Ralph Waldo Emerson

Brené Brown grew up in a household with extremely high expectations of success and perfection. She constantly felt pressure to meet unrealistic goals, adhere to external standards, and prove her worth according to her parents' ideology. This led her to a successful career in academia - eventually becoming a research professor at the University of Houston, where she studied vulnerability, courage, shame, and empathy. Despite her achievements, Brené couldn't shake a lingering sense of inadequacy or the overwhelming drive to keep excelling.

In 2006, she hit a turning point. While conducting her research, Brené realized that vulnerability lies at the core of meaningful human experiences - but it's also the heart of fear and shame. That insight triggered a personal crisis, exposing her own struggles. Through therapy, she confronted her fears and insecurities, learning that she had used her perfectionist drive to shield herself from the pain of vulnerability. This realization became the cornerstone of her work. In 2010, she shared her journey and findings in her TEDx talk, "The Power of Vulnerability," which went viral and resonated with millions. Brené ultimately broke free from societal pressures, embraced her true self, and emerged as a leading voice on vulnerability and courage. Her story demonstrates that by challenging societal norms, we can defeat Social Debt and lead a fulfilling, authentic life.

Defining Social Debt

Social Debt is an emotional state where you accumulate negative social experiences. For years, I felt the silent condemnation from my family insisting I 'should have kids.' The guilt weighed on me. I was still trying to find meaning in my own life but had to face family questions at every gathering. That's pure Social Debt, and it's exhausting. It exists because society creates and reinforces "acceptable" behaviors, rules, and moral principles - this has been true throughout history, across nearly all cultures. We agree on ways to operate and survive together, establishing social guidelines to simplify daily life. Many of these rules eventually disappear or change over time.

But whenever you break them - intentionally or not - you create Social Debt. You often sense it the moment it happens, sometimes even physically. Your mind then wrestles with the social system, generating feelings like guilt, anger, ignorance, or numbness, all of which add up in your internal "Social Debt meta-bank." With hundreds or thousands of such rules around, it's guaranteed that you'll face daily pressure to behave in certain ways.

Struggling with Social Debt starts early, as soon as you begin interacting with people. Your "meta-bank" is constantly adding or subtracting "social credits." Gaps in your social knowledge - like missing certain cues or lacking basic etiquette - might make others laugh at you or even humiliate you, which only increases the debt you carry.

Paying off Social Debt is exhausting. Shame is often at the core, as Brené discovered. You find yourself torn between caring about people's judgments and respecting their norms, or accepting your own reality and defying the status quo. Yes, meditation, affirmations, and self-awareness can help reduce some stress in the moment, but on a broader level, they're rarely enough to clear this debt completely.

To really improve, you need to dissect the structure of your own Social Debt and apply strategic, holistic approaches to reduce how much control other people have over you. This doesn't mean rebelling against every rule - you just need a practical system to manage its impact.

Three Forms of Social Debt

Expected Behavior: You've probably noticed that everyone has opinions on what you should or shouldn't do - covering nearly every aspect of life. While this may have logical roots, a lot of interactions are borderline absurd. My parents would say, "You can't do that," and if I asked "Why?" they'd reply, "Because I said so." Multiply that by thousands of scenarios. For example, being invited to a dinner party but not bringing a bottle of wine - society labels that as impolite. You've ignored a social expectation, and now you feel guilty, adding points to your Social Debt bank, like you would deposit money in your real bank. With such a powerful judgment system in place, it's easy for others to manipulate your life. Instead of making aware and conscious decisions, you're overwhelmed by external pressures, unsure how to handle them, so you retreat to familiar - often unhealthy - comfort habits.

Attention Deprivation: We're social creatures and can become deeply dependent on other people's opinions. Look at social media for proof: people will do almost anything to get likes and followers, often losing themselves in the process. That's also why many of us have forgotten how to enjoy time alone. When you crave attention, your Social Debt skyrockets. Even if you're introverted, you may still seek validation - verbally or nonverbally. Mix that with Expected Behavior, and you have a risky combo - a drive to do anything to feel "seen" and to justify your existence.

Social Acceptance: While it's great to learn to be alone, plenty of people feel lonely even in crowded spaces. With so many external expectations and the chase for attention, sometimes all we want is for someone to understand and accept us for who we are. Ironically, the harder we seek acceptance, the more we lose our authenticity. Historically, tribal communities held initiation ceremonies for new members; it mattered for group survival and was used to create a shared sense of belonging. Today, we technically need less from others, but our craving for social acceptance is still strong. When we can't find it, we turn to artificial replacements - feeding our loneliness with impulsive choices. We envy the relationships others have and try different forms of escape. My own favorite is travel. There's nothing wrong with exploring other places and cultures, but sometimes it's just a way to run from emotional isolation. You can stand on top of the highest mountain and still feel miserable. Combine this with Expected Behavior and Attention Deprivation, and your Social Debt becomes practically unpayable without a major psychological breakthrough.

When you fall short of people's expectations, struggle to find a supportive community, or suffer from inadequate attention and recognition, you'll likely drown in Social Debt. Add typical life stressors - health issues, money problems, family drama - and you're primed for a personal crisis. It would be easier to handle if you only had to manage your own debt, but it's never that simple. Everyone else carries their own Social Debt, which spills over into your life through unhealthy ripple effects.

Steps Toward Reducing Social Debt

Improving your Personal Maturity can reduce most Social Debt challenges. I suggest documenting the moments you feel socially indebted for a couple of weeks. Track recurring triggers - it'll reveal your weak spots and the underlying reasons. Later on, we'll discuss more detailed solutions, but for now, just keep the big picture in mind. You don't have to ditch social norms entirely - you just need to develop a personality strong enough to navigate them without becoming trapped by them.

Here are a few basic principles to start your recovery journey:

- Acceptance: Learn to accept the complexity of the world and let go of responsibility for factors you can't control. In Section 4, I'll discuss Radical Acceptance as part of a broader "Radical Philosophy." Acceptance lets you respond creatively to new and ongoing Social Debt scenarios, helping you maintain a positive mindset.

- Communication: We communicate by speaking, reading, writing, thinking, and - most importantly - listening. Mastering all five drastically improves social engagement and your ability to understand and be understood. One person might be a great thinker but a poor listener; another might excel at reading and writing but stumble in face-to-face conversations. That gap breeds negative experiences. However, if you pair acceptance with a desire to refine your communication skills, you'll expand your influence on other individuals, your community, and even entire nations.

- Efficiency: Your effectiveness grows as you grasp the nuances of how we live and how to maneuver different hierarchies. Societies often revolve around Dominance Hierarchies. Strong communication skills, plus the ability to accept challenges, will help you build an internal system to function more effectively - even if you're not high on the social totem pole. Without some form of hierarchy, survival would be more complicated; your job is to figure out how to navigate these structures without letting them crush you.

The goal is to continuously reduce any existing debt while minimizing the buildup of new debt. You'll apply these principles to the three Social Debt categories:

- Debt of Expected Behavior: The simplest shortcut is to find a mentor who can teach you how to handle societal expectations, navigate dominance hierarchies, and improve your communication. A good mentor will point out social interactions you might overlook, helping you accumulate new, positive experiences. And don't forget - you can also become a mentor for someone else.

- Debt of Attention Deprivation: Extroverts and introverts should learn from each other. By combining acceptance and communication, you'll better grasp different perspectives as well as your own needs. Chances are, social media won't give you what you need - it might be about finally stepping outside for a walk.

- Debt of Social Acceptance: This one is cultural at its core. Unless society as a whole decides to change, each of us must work on our individual behaviors. This is mostly a psychological process - accepting that not everyone will like you, and doing so without damaging your ego. The moment you can handle that, you start moving from "red" to "black" in your Social Debt bank.

While you wrestle with the Follower's Mindset and Borrowed Success, society keeps piling on more expectations. That raises your Social Debt even more as you absorb new rules, norms, and scrutiny - most of which nobody taught you how to handle until it was too late. Remember how I said I felt ten years behind everyone socially and constantly found myself in awkward situations? That's how Social Debt can manifest. You do or say something dumb and realize years later how embarrassing it was. If you add proper parenting, friendship, structured teaching, and practice, it's easier to avoid such pitfalls. Some call it "street smarts," and we praise those who have it, but it should be the baseline. Instead, we often create social disconnections, leaving people to fend for themselves. Some manage to survive; others vanish in the chaos.

I recall my first job interview for a Quality Assurance Engineer position in 2009. I had no idea how interviews worked, what to say, or how to act. Sure, you could argue it was a character-building experience, but if I'd had a bit more guidance, maybe I wouldn't have suggested redesigning the entire corporate website to the interviewer. The company had thousands of employees, likely with an entire team dedicated to web design, and Quality Assurance had nothing to do with it. Looking back, I realize I was desperate to impress. It was my first interview, but I failed, and they never called. A year later, I tried again for the same role at the same company and got hired - but to this day, I still cringe remembering that first attempt. That's Social Debt - small but lodged deep.

Another example: I physically shudder when I remember this. One day in New York, I was walking downtown in a bad mood. Two older homeless men were walking toward me. We collided, shoulder to shoulder - a normal occurrence on busy streets. I turned around, about to say something. One of them had been carrying a plate of food, and as we bumped, he dropped it all. He stared at the spilled food, clearly upset, maybe trying to say something but couldn't. I took one look at him, then the mess on the ground, and just walked away. At first, I felt annoyed - like he should've been more careful. Maybe ten minutes later, the gravity of what I'd done hit me. I felt sickened by my own behavior and my initial reaction. His face still haunts me. I don't know if I can ever repay that debt; maybe I shouldn't.

Stories like these, big or small, are a slow death by a thousand cuts. You're expected to abide by unwritten rules, handle a lack of attention and recognition, and not be shocked when society disapproves of your uniqueness. Social Debt can feel infinite, and the Follower's Mindset only makes it worse. Despite all the pressure, you're still expected to win, enjoy the "game," and become successful. The easiest way is to Borrow someone else's Success, which gives a fleeting sense of accomplishment but often leaves you feeling empty. Many realize too late that this approach doesn't work.

As Brené Brown reminds us, embracing vulnerability and letting go of shame is how we reduce - and ultimately free ourselves from - Social Debt.

You've been given almost no alternatives besides repeating other people's paths, building Borrowed Success stories, and celebrating "fake" achievements. You're forced into the Follower's Mindset, stacking up Social Debt in the process. Everything is monitored and scrutinized, leaving you few exits. You've been dropped into a reality where "fake" is praised and "real" is punished, and everyone wants to sell you a quick fix that promises a better life. You'll never get there unless you understand - and change - your Fundamental Reality.

Now, let's sort out the final piece of the puzzle. We need to see why so many people lose their sense of purpose. Up next: Fundamental Reality.

CHAPTER 5

FUNDAMENTAL REALITY

> *"Pain is inevitable. Suffering is optional."*
> - Haruki Murakami

Have you ever taken a sip of a hot drink without realizing it was hot? You feel pain and a bit foolish, and while it might not change your life, it teaches you a decent lesson. Now, imagine being shot in the head - that's an entirely different level of pain.

Malala Yousafzai, a young Pakistani girl, experienced exactly that on her way home from school. Under the Taliban regime, girls were banned from attending school. Despite ongoing threats and an oppressive environment, Malala refused to give up her education and continued to advocate for girls' rights to learn. The Taliban targeted her for her activism, leaving her in critical condition. She managed to escape to the United Kingdom for treatment, and rather than being silenced, she fought back even harder. Malala began speaking on a global stage, addressed the United Nations, and created the Malala Fund to champion girls' education worldwide. She became the youngest person to receive the Nobel Peace Prize, inspiring millions with her unwavering dedication to ensuring that every girl has the right to an education.

You can't ignore pain. You can learn from it or become its victim - and I don't recommend the latter. Pain is an undeniable part of life. Though it's hard to handle, it can shape your character and make you more resilient. In severe cases, like losing a loved one, pain may envelop you in grief and suffering for a long time. But no matter its source, experiencing pain usually means you're standing on the wrong side - an opposite of where you naturally want to be. It's mysterious, even incomprehensible: It can take everything from you one day, then spark positive change the next. Pain avoidance is a losing strategy. People like Malala learn that pain can be managed, even in the most oppressive environments, and through it, they find renewed purpose.

Pain is part of Fundamental Reality. It draws the line between being a leader or clinging to a Follower's Mindset, between chasing Life Purpose or settling for empty Borrowed Success, and between getting buried in Social Debt or confidently making transformative choices. Ultimately, facing pain - physical or emotional - can guide you toward a meaningful life. And it's not just pain; other core elements of Fundamental Reality - like truth, fear, hope, and sacrifice - can do the same. The key is accepting reality and figuring out how to use it in your favor.

Malala's story shows how adversity can shape a purposeful life and how confronting Fundamental Reality leads to Growth and meaningful impact. But practicing self-development to deal with emotional and physical pain isn't a shortcut to easy solutions. I learned this the hard way.

In 2022, I wanted to run a marathon. I'd played soccer as a kid, so I assumed running long distances would be simple. I was wrong. Running more than 5 kilometers proved to be tough, so I started to train properly. Each time I aimed for a new milestone - 8 km, 10 km, 15 km - my body rebelled, and my mind tried to talk me out of it. It felt physically and mentally impossible. I got injured a few times, and each injury briefly "excused" me from running. But then I felt guilty for giving up, so I kept coming back - this went on for two years. Every time I completed that next "impossible" distance, I felt a psychological release. During those long runs, I realized my mind might be stronger than my body, but both would sabotage me in the name of survival. My solution was to become curious about pain management. I accepted that maybe I'd never finish a marathon, but I wanted to see what would happen if I didn't stop. One day, I ran 30 km and thought, "Wow, remember when I believed 10 km was too painful?" Then, in February 2024, I planned a 35-km training run but felt different that day - I just decided to keep going. Just like that, on a random day, I finished my first marathon. I went home, sat on the couch, and couldn't believe it. All those runs, the resistance, the fear, and the doubt were part of the Transformation. Maybe I got lucky, but it's also true that character development is a slow, painful process. You can't cut out the darkness; you learn to harness it. The more you apply critical thinking, the more you see how understanding Fundamental Reality influences your life choices.

This journey is long and difficult because life is split into drastically different elements - like "Life in the Nutshell" - and we struggle to piece it together on our own, even though we do agree on certain common-sense ideas. We can't just google our unique purpose for living. The key lies in how we perceive Fundamental Reality, tied closely to our ability to manage consciousness and interpret subconscious messages. It's the ultimate challenge - it often seems impossible, hopeless, or unbearable, which is why many choose to live with pain, numbing it through dopamine spikes or other artificial means, ultimately losing sight of their Life Purpose.

Every aspect of Fundamental Reality - like pain - is part of a bigger, ever-expanding system, similar to how the universe itself keeps expanding. It grows with each meaningful experience we create, with every new rule society imposes (and the resulting Social Debt), and each time someone shatters the barrier of what's "impossible" (like completing a marathon or traveling to space). To navigate this ongoing evolution, we need personal frameworks that help us process assumptions, rules, and challenges using critical thinking and feedback loops.

So what happens when Fundamental Reality changes? The "truth" we relied on can suddenly become obsolete. Many people resist this new reality simply because they haven't developed critical thinking skills. If truth keeps shifting, can the world stay at peace? Without a reason to exist, truth is pointless; it matters only when there's unfulfilled potential or great value to be found on the other side of the challenge.

We also have to factor in opposing forces within Fundamental Reality. The opposite of pain is pleasure, which people often confuse with happiness. Having these extremes might suggest balance, but in my view, that balance isn't a midpoint it's different for everyone. If the middle is numbness, who wants that? Instead of seeking some mystical "balance," we should find our own paths - a personal journey to purpose. Along this path, we use failure and hardship to build strength and discipline; we let pleasure illuminate rather than spoil us; and we transform into someone whose wisdom can help others.

Life is about constant trade-offs, oscillating between extremes, and inching toward our true north. Consider childbirth - intense pain precedes the joy of raising a child.

The faster we recognize how Fundamental Reality operates, the sooner we can tackle Follower's Mindset, Social Debt, and Borrowed Success. A few key concepts (Figure 2) lie at the heart of this understanding, providing clarity and direction:

- Dominance Hierarchy (from Jordan Peterson) – A layered framework that includes your Ego (personal ambition and self-awareness), the Social environment (rules and relationships), and Nature (external realities we can't fully control).

- The Golden Circle (from Simon Sinek) – A structure that starts with "Why" (purpose and motivation), followed by "How" (process), and ending with "What" (tangible results).

- Behavior Change (from James Clear) – Centered on gradual improvement through habit formation, identity shifts, and smart environmental design.

Fundamental Reality

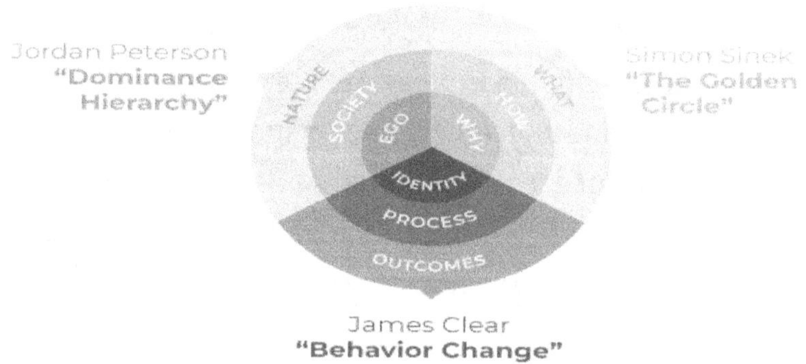

Figure 2. "Three concepts of Fundamental Reality"

While it might not be obvious yet, these ideas tie in with everything we've covered so far. Dominance Hierarchy grounds us in social and natural realities. The Golden Circle aligns our deeper motivations with practical outcomes. Behavior Change provides an iterative blueprint for reaching and sustaining our purpose.

At the center of everything is you - your ego. By asking tough questions through critical thinking (like "Why am I here?") and facing the challenges of Fundamental Reality, you shape your identity and develop a Growth Mindset. Beyond you is society, with its cultures, rules, and obligations that impose Social Debt. Society demands you engage in well-defined processes (e.g., securing an income) and also influences you toward a Follower's Mindset or Borrowed Success. Above society is nature and the forces beyond our control. Understanding which battles you can and can't fight becomes clearer here. When your ego answers the Why and How, your identity can guide you toward fulfilling actions.

At this scale, it's also about the powers we're still researching, and the unknown frontiers we haven't conquered. One thing is certain: If we ignore nature too long, it will eventually crush us.

Your unique path toward Personal Maturity lies hidden somewhere within these layers. You've been given the freedom to explore, experiment, and evolve throughout our lives. Change and Transformation are crucial to your identity, and you need a dynamic blend of inner work and outer action to progress. Several elements of Fundamental Reality serve as tools for this Transformation:

- Pain reminds us of the inevitable and pushes us to make life-changing decisions.
- Truth is a radical form of trust, letting us revisit and revise our beliefs.

- Fear signals that we're on the wrong path, prompting us to course-correct and conquer obstacles.

- Hope is a subconscious kindness, urging us to uplift those who have lost it.

- Sacrifice is aligning with a greater cause, guiding us to choose our battles wisely.

Each element requires accepting a world that's complicated, ever-shifting, and full of unknowns. Character development starts when you fully acknowledge this reality and learn to apply these truths. You'll never achieve perfect "balance" - only a path of creation and Growth, sometimes veering from one extreme to the other, aiming for what feels like your true north.

Fundamental Reality makes you aware of behavior patterns, social structures, emotional states, and processes that affect your Personal Maturity. When you're locked in a Follower's Mindset, heavy with Social Debt, and chasing Borrowed Success, your Fundamental Reality looks dramatically different from the reality of someone who embraces life with genuine meaning. For a person grounded in strong character, a Growth Mindset, a clear Vision, solid Values, and guiding principles, there's a real opportunity to design life on their own terms.

Now that we've built enough awareness, it's time to start our journey toward discovering Life Purpose and exploring Life Design.

SECTION 2 - LIFE PURPOSE

"It is never too late to be what you might have been."

— George Eliot

"**I**'m aware that life is hard. How is this awareness going to help me find my purpose?"

I'm glad you asked. I had the same question about 17 years ago when I started delving into psychology to understand the subconscious mind - how it shapes my behavior, habits, health, and everything else in life. My own learning process was intense, marked by mistakes, disappointments, and revelations. Yours might be more enjoyable. That's why I'm sharing all the knowledge and wisdom I've accumulated along the way - summarized here to better equip you to face your Fundamental Reality. My hope is that this book will simplify your search for meaning and give you the courage to discover your

Life Purpose. Maybe, down the road, you'll decide to help someone else - either by guiding them yourself or by handing them this book.

Over the years, I've been tackling the challenges described in Section 1 without even realizing it. I bounced from one personal issue to another while climbing the career ladder, trying to be more socially responsible, and spending countless hours questioning my own existence - always asking "Why?" Eventually, I noticed that every time I achieved something meaningful, I went through a sort of "reset." It's like flipping a reality switch: In a split second, you become a different person, and there's no going back. These resets can come from devastating experiences or fulfilling ones. I began documenting them and celebrating each one. The truth is, they can happen anywhere, anytime, and we have zero control over when or how. I recorded all my insights and grouped them into logical blocks, which eventually turned into the concept I call Personal Maturity. We've discussed this topic a bit already and we'll explore it in detail in Section 3, but for now, let's turn our attention to self-discovery.

Cheryl Strayed lost her sense of purpose after her mother died of cancer. Her life spiraled into chaos, her marriage fell apart, and she increasingly relied on destructive coping mechanisms. She soon reached a breaking point and realized she needed a drastic change. What did she do? She went on a hike - specifically, the Pacific Crest Trail, logging over a thousand miles through harsh wilderness despite having almost no hiking experience. Her goal was to heal and rediscover herself. Predictably, she endured extreme weather, physical fatigue, and isolation. Still, she persevered, and the journey allowed her to process her grief, forgive herself for past mistakes, and find peace. She chronicled her experiences in her memoir, Wild: From Lost to Found on the Pacific Crest Trail, which became a bestseller and inspired many to pursue their own paths.

You're about to embark on a self-discovery journey, too. It may not look like Cheryl's, but it could feel just as intense, because Life Purpose - one of the elements of Fundamental Reality, like pain or fear - requires real work. It's crucial for living meaningfully, fueling our adventures. It's also the ultimate sacrifice: the bigger your purpose, the greater the sacrifice needed to achieve it. As we saw in Chapter 1, the alternative can be a dark maze of heavy expectations, social disappointments, and chasing someone else's Dream.

Your journey toward finding and fulfilling your Life Purpose will be influenced by the Follower's Mindset, Borrowed Success, and Social Debt. By building awareness - like we discussed in Chapter 1 - you'll improve your odds of conquering these hurdles. Staying conscious of your challenges and inner conflicts is key to your success.

According to the concept of Personal Maturity, defining your purpose means developing a Vision, Mission, Values, Qualities, and Identities. For now, these might just sound like words, but in this section, we'll break down each in detail. Each chapter in Section 2 will guide you through discovering your Life Purpose. By the end, you should have a far clearer sense of who and where you are in life. In short, we're doing Life Design, which can pave the way for greatness.

Let's begin with Vision.

CHAPTER 6

VISION

> *"A man's worth is no greater than the worth of his ambitions."*
>
> **- Marcus Aurelius**

Life is painfully empty without a Dream. Every remarkable journey starts with one.

Dreaming big is the first step toward freeing yourself from the Follower's Mindset, Social Debt, and Borrowed Success. It's like testing the hypothesis of something impossible until you make it real. People will say, "Don't do it," while your gut insists, "They're wrong." Dreaming big shapes your Vision and stress-tests how passionate you are about bringing your aims to life. It can convert Vision into reality and mold your Values and character, which you'll need to live a life brimming with extraordinary experiences.

In Section 1, we built enough awareness to see that life is a complex ecosystem governed by various patterns and existential "rules." We humans know a lot about the world - and yet, in the grand scheme, we know very little. This gap offers us the freedom to shape our lives in almost any way we choose. You can unearth the unknown and share it with everyone else. But first, you have to unearth yourself. Think of it this way (Figure 3):

- Living life with purpose is possible when you define a great Vision.

- Defining a great Vision is possible only when you Dream big.

- Dreaming big is possible only through high Personal Maturity.

- High Personal Maturity is achieved through meaningful experience.

- Meaningful experience arises from a self-discovery journey.

Figure 3. "Logical Journey to a great Vision"

So I encourage you to set out on yours.

Ultimately, the quality of your Life Purpose hinges on the lessons you learn, actions you take, and improvements you make based on real-world experience.

You can treat self-discovery like a personal development project (Figure 4). You'll succeed by carving out time to think, reflect, and practice. There's no deadline; you might even find it's an ongoing process. The first time I did this, it took me about three months to go through the steps I'll describe below.

Figure 4. "Step by step process for Self-Discovery"

- Start: Write down every Big Dream that comes to your mind - anything that feels exciting or compelling.

- Explore: Cultivate curiosity about your Dream and Vision. Ask others if they have Vision or Big Dream and how they found them. Look at the world through fresh eyes, explore new types of information, and gather diverse opinions so you can discover insights in them.

- Reflect: Set aside regular time to review your findings. Notice how different or even controversial perspectives affect you. Learn to navigate challenging discussions without experiencing negative fallout. You might not have a clear Vision yet, but remain open to revelations.

- Experiment: Try new experiences, both small and significant, that shake up your routine and make you question your reality - volunteering, a new hobby, or switching jobs, for instance.

- Analyze: Pay attention to activities or moments that spark satisfaction or a sense of achievement. Document everything. These observations can offer big clues about the Dream and Vision you want to pursue.

- Support: Seek a mentor, coach, counselor, or anyone who can offer professional insights and guide you in crystallizing your Dream - and eventually your Vision.

- Lock: Dream evolve, so make a habit of self-reflection at least once a year.

Armed with at least a few Big Dream, you can start brainstorming your Vision. Think of your Vision as a self-agreement about the life you want. You might not yet know how or what you'll do, but you want to be crystal-clear on why you're doing it. I once stayed two years longer in a marriage I already knew was broken, ignoring the big picture. Why? Because I felt society expected me to "make it work." I lost sight of my own Vision - until the quiet misery became unbearable. When I finally left, it was like stepping back onto my true path.

A Vision reflects your potential to pull off the impossible. It's fueled by your unique talents and skills, and it requires casting aside self-limiting beliefs - like those tied to Social Debt - along with your doubts, fears, and negativity. A Vision paints the picture of a great future, and Dreaming big helps you see that future in 5, 10, or even 20 years. You should visualize your ambitions and then commit them to paper. Once you do, your Creator's Mindset activates - this powerful state lets you imagine and define your own version of existence.

Your first Vision doesn't have to be massive; it just needs to be yours. Maybe you'll Dream "to make life on Mars possible," or maybe you'll Dream "to keep my parents' farm thriving." Whatever it is, write it down without letting fear or doubt step in. The moment you do, you'll feel a flash of clarity - like it's already a bit more real. And it is. That's the satisfaction of deciding for yourself. Later, you can assemble a team of people who'll help make it happen. The right people will challenge your Dream and Vision, but they won't try to destroy them.

Keep in mind there are as many potential Visions as there are stars in the sky - and likely more. That means no single formula exists for creating one. It's up for interpretation, though common frameworks do exist. Some people form Visions based on religion, others on science or psychology, and still others on social or philosophical principles. Those ideas can shape the direction and tone of your Vision, but at the end of the day, it's still the unique perspective of one individual: You.

In 2006, while traveling through Argentina, Blake Mycoskie noticed many children growing up without shoes - more than just an inconvenience, it was a health hazard. Injuries and infections from going barefoot kept kids out of school and disrupted their lives. On returning home to the U.S., Blake launched TOMS Shoes with an almost impossible idea: "One for One" - for every pair sold, another pair would be donated to a child in need. This bold Vision led to steep challenges with investors and distributors. The logistics seemed impossible. But a great Vision, powered by genuine passion, can succeed against the odds. Blake stuck with it, focusing on his simple yet powerful goal: improving the lives of children in need. Eventually,

TOMS distributed millions of shoes to kids in over 60 countries, and his concept of a socially responsible business inspired countless others. He dared to Dream big and forged a Vision that changed the world. That's something any Dreamer can do.

Dreaming big, revisiting your Vision, and improving it is a skill that grows over time. You should revisit your Vision at least once a year because it will shape the other components of your Life Purpose, which we'll discuss throughout this section. To make your subsequent reflections more fruitful, keep broadening your knowledge of the universe and take tangible steps, however small, to move your Vision forward. Celebrate each micro-change or small win you achieve (We'll talk about this more in Section 4).

As we dig into more elements of Life Purpose, you'll see how everything ties together. Purpose is a mindset shaped by certain building blocks, and the first one is Vision. It's almost impossible to experience real meaning in life without a clear Vision - yet you can't form that Vision without a Big Dream. The challenge is to learn how to reach a Creator's Mindset through meaningful experiences and self-discovery.

Once you have a Vision, you can seek out a Mission that brings you closer to realizing it.

Let's talk about your Mission next.

CHAPTER 7

MISSION

> *"Efforts and courage are not enough without purpose and direction."*
>
> - John F. Kennedy

It's time to find a quest for your Vision.

We call it a Mission Statement. Having one is vital; having many is extraordinary. Your Mission Statement explains how you can achieve your Vision - a form of long-term goal. It should offer enough detail to guide you, especially when you face tough decisions. The main challenge is figuring out how to discover, choose, document, and then act on a Mission Statement.

Vision and Mission - terms popular in business - often show up in motivational speeches, self-help books, and philosophical discussions. Despite the flood of information, many people still struggle to define their own Mission or connect it to their Vision. For instance, if your Vision is "to make it possible to live on Mars," what's the right Mission for such an ambitious idea? Would you do it by creating technology to improve space travel, reduce radiation exposure, or to make landings safer? Maybe your strategy involves changing international law. You have lots of options. The trick is having a Mission Statement you can act on now.

A good Mission Statement should be motivational - strong enough to help you break free from Social Debt, the Follower's Mindset, and Borrowed Success. Without clear direction, people often cope by escaping reality - adopting a nomadic lifestyle, rebelling, or even drifting toward crime. We all find ways to run from our problems. But if you have a documented Vision and Mission, you're more likely to stay committed. There's a kind of magic in knowing exactly what you want and why.

Scott Harrison envisioned solving the global water crisis. He decided the best way for him to achieve this was to found a charity called "Water." (Excellent branding, by the way.) The idea took shape during his volunteer work as a photojournalist on a hospital ship off the coast of Liberia. He witnessed extreme poverty firsthand and realized how critical access to clean water was for people in developing nations.

What led him there? Before this, Scott lived a life of excess as a nightclub promoter in New York City. He was drowning in a hedonistic lifestyle and felt unfulfilled, suspecting there had to be more. That inner turmoil pushed him to make a drastic decision, which gave him a meaningful new purpose. In 2006, he launched Charity: Water, a nonprofit dedicated to bringing clean drinking water to communities in need. Using his promotional skills, he built a compelling narrative and brand around the cause. Like Blake Mycoskie with TOMS, Scott faced donors who were skeptical, plus huge logistical hurdles. But obstacles didn't deter him. He introduced creative fundraising tactics - like asking people to donate their birthdays - and built a transparent model: 100% of public donations went straight to water projects. Today, Charity: Water has funded more than 64,000 water projects in 29 countries, helping over 13 million people. It's a testament to the power of Vision plus a specific Mission. Not many nightclub promoters go on to improve the world on this scale, yet Scott pulled it off because he believed in something big, which made him strong enough to eclipse the inertia of Social Debt, Borrowed Success, and the Follower's Mindset.

Why a Mission Statement?

A Mission Statement is your roadmap, translating an abstract Vision into a tangible reality. It's not a new concept, but it's rarely applied seriously. People say, "It's just words on paper," but they're wrong. All parts of your Life Purpose - including your Mission - are powerful tools. This is your life, not a casual sideshow. Identifying and committing to a unique Mission can be uncomfortable or even scary, which is why many stick to Borrowed Success so they have something to celebrate. I'm not here to shame you if you'd rather follow a tried-and-true success playbook instead of writing your own - but deep down, you might be happier creating your own path. A Mission Statement shouldn't be a random list of jargon or a copy-paste from a celebrity entrepreneur's bio. It needs to be personal - a genuine commitment to your Vision. Every choice and action you take flows from it, keeping you on track even when other options pop up. The hardest part is taking that initial step.

How to Build Your Mission Statement

I will share with you simple yet practical steps to create your Mission Statement (Figure 5).

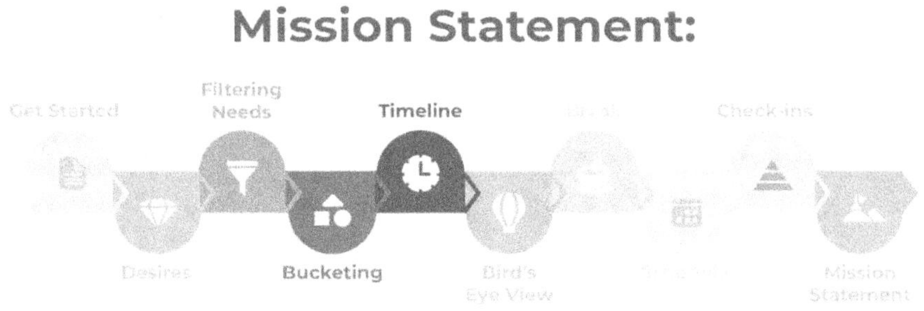

Figure 5. "Steps to build Mission Statement"

- Get Started: Write something down - anything that could serve as a Mission Statement connected to your Vision. This is just your first step, so it doesn't have to be perfect. Does it look noble? Does it need to be? Whether your first attempt is bold or modest, put it on paper. You might experience real resistance - mostly psychological - as your comfort-loving mind tries to talk you out of it. That's normal.

- Desires: Put your draft statement aside for a moment. List all the tangible and intangible things you want from life. No limits - your list could have 10 items or 1,000. (I've done this before and ended up with over 1,500!) Spend a few weeks jotting down 10–15 items a day. That's how you clear mental clutter. Among the junk, you'll find gems that can validate and refine your Mission Statement.

- Filtering Needs: Once you have a decent list, split it into "Things I want" vs. "Things I need." The "need" side often represents Social Debt or obligations you don't genuinely desire but feel you must fulfill to avoid societal or interpersonal repercussions. The "want" side are items you truly crave - possibly crucial for reaching your Vision. You might feel uneasy admitting you want them, but that's okay. Your aim here is to be brutally honest. Most of the time, "Things I want" is just 10–20% of the entire list, which means you're heavily tied up in someone else's agenda via "Things I need." Look for ways to reduce or eliminate "needs" that aren't absolutely necessary (and won't harm anyone if you drop them).

- Bucketing: Group items into categories like Business, Family, Hobby, and Transformation - or any set of categories that mirror your life. Notice if one category overshadows the others. How does that connect to your Vision and initial Mission Statement? If there's no correlation, that's a sign you need to rebalance.

- Timeline: Attach timeframes to each item: 1 month, 3 months, or 6 months; 1 year, 2 years, or 3 years; 5 years, 10 years, or 25 years. This can be challenging but extremely helpful in figuring out your priorities. Often, things you genuinely want end up stuck behind "needs" in the 5–10-year range. Translation: They'll never happen because you're busy with other people's demands. You'll likely see how the Follower's Mindset, Social Debt, and Borrowed Success have seeped into your list. You can keep some but not all.

- Bird's Eye View: Step back and look for patterns. Are you overloading on hobbies to escape reality? Are you neglecting family or personal Growth in favor of business? Remember, your Vision can be anything. "Being the greatest dad on Earth" is a fantastic Vision if it's coupled with a solid Mission. It might be tough to become the first at it globally, but it's still a legitimate path. This broader perspective reveals unhealthy habits or categories dominating your list. Keep removing or revising whatever doesn't align with your Vision and Mission.

- Break: Take a few weeks off, then revisit the list for a fresh perspective. That will be a good time to share what you've done with friends or family. Seek support but don't expect a miracle - this is your journey, and you're fully responsible for it.

- Schedule: Move as many "want" items as possible - those that align with your first Mission Statement - into a 1–12-month window. Start making progress on them. This will require life changes, so pace yourself. (We'll cover best practices in Section 4.)

- Check-ins: Review your list monthly. Keep nudging the "wants" forward. This step helps you get real-time feedback on your emotional state and whether you enjoy the path you're on. Document both your progress and how you feel.

- Mission Statement: After 6–12 months of acting on these "want" items, you'll have a clearer sense of whether your initial Mission Statement still holds. Maybe it's perfect; maybe it needs a rewrite. There's no secret formula - this is trial and error.

A Mission Statement doesn't need to be perfect from day one, nor do you want to rewrite it every other week. It should be impactful enough to hold up for at least a year of real-world testing. Ultimately, this is about designing your life, and that's no quick fix but it's powerful, setting you up for a huge adventure.

Evolving Vision & Mission

Both your Vision and Mission will evolve as time goes on. The more space you give them to grow, the more confident you'll be in their significance. A Mission Statement adds a storyline to your life, maintaining stability amid the chaos and nudging you toward action.

Vision and Mission open the door to self-discovery in a practical, hands-on way. This is where you uncover who you truly are. You can approach self-discovery systematically, as outlined in this chapter, which helps break painful cycles. Over time, each Mission you undertake builds new skills, momentum, and hard-earned wisdom to guide your future decisions. It also pushes you to think hard about what you truly value because you'll make choices that may dramatically change who you are and what you do. It's a snapshot of who you're becoming - an exceptional person who fears nothing because you're on a Mission to …? (That's for you to decide.)

Up next, we'll explore Values.

CHAPTER 8

VALUES

> *"It's not hard to make decisions when you know what your Values are."*
>
> — Roy E. Disney

What do you value most? Trust, respect, money, or your reputation? Only a person with strong personal Values can pursue their Vision and Mission effectively. You have to look inward and embark on a self-discovery journey to unearth those Values - because life will confront you with some truly heavy decisions.

Nick Vujicic is living proof of this. You might know him as a motivational speaker born without arms or legs - a challenge of staggering proportions. Nick endured physical hardships from childhood, faced relentless bullying, battled severe depression, and found himself questioning his very purpose. Everything changed when he embraced his reality and perceived his condition not as a barrier but as a launching pad. He developed a set of core Values that have driven his actions and inspired millions around the globe - especially Values centered on helping others. Imagine that: A man without arms and legs finds his calling in serving others. Nick began sharing his story and encouraging people to overcome their own struggles. He traveled the world, speaking in schools, churches, and conferences, delivering a message of hope and resilience. He founded Life Without Limbs to offer resources for people in similar circumstances. Today, Nick is an internationally renowned motivational speaker and author. His impact is enormous, and it all stems from living out his core Values:

- Faith: Trusting that life has meaning beyond physical limitations.

- Resilience: Viewing challenges as opportunities for Growth.

- Compassion: Understanding others' struggles and offering support.

- Integrity: Staying true to his principles and beliefs.

- Positivity: Focusing on Life positives and maintaining an optimistic outlook.

When you have well-defined Values, you're able to clarify why, how, and what you do. They can also inspire others to join you on your Mission - just like Nick has done. Essentially, Values are your ideology, beliefs, and philosophy wrapped into a handful of simple statements. You're designing a life filled with purpose, after all.

I've spent years discovering my own core Values: Simplicity, Health, Meaning, Wisdom, Freedom. Sure, they might look like a random collection of words, but together, they form a powerful guiding principle for my life: I continuously simplify my life to focus on health and meaningful experiences so that I can generate wisdom to share with others and reach absolute freedom to be effective on my Mission and get closer to my purpose.

For instance, I chose Health because I spent most of my life battling digestive issues - two stomach ulcers, constant headaches, back pain, and general fatigue. I was basically on a permanent medication schedule, taking multiple pills a day. It was miserable. Sometimes I felt sorry for myself and played the victim. Then in 2018, I decided this just wasn't sustainable. I quit the meds, dived into research on alternative healing methods, experimented with different foods, learned about fasting, and put all the theories I found to the test. I remember doing a seven-day water fast. The first days were hell: my heart rate was around 140 bpm all the time, I was drenched in sweat, and I could barely sleep. By day four, my body adapted - I felt almost peaceful, and my food cravings disappeared. I even worked out a bit. When the fast finally ended, I had no desire to eat. I felt so light, so mentally clear. The smell of cooking meat on a food truck made me gag - it was unbelievably intense. I noticed that my Vision got sharper, and I no longer had stomach pain. Over six months, I healed my ulcers, and my blood pressure dropped from 130/90 to 110/70. My doctors were stunned. I learned that when you're ill, it's hard to focus on anything other than feeling better, often slipping into a victim mentality and seeking pity from others. There's no space for a Big Dream in that state. But once I recovered, everything shifted. I stopped taking health for granted and made it a core element of my lifestyle.

When your Values align with your Vision and Mission, it all starts to click. You'll have a solid framework for making life decisions - like my health experiments. Values are critical to life design, preventing you from getting lost in the Follower's Mindset, accumulating Social Debt, or chasing Borrowed Success.

Discovering Your Values

You completed a 10-step exercise in Chapter 7, producing a substantial list of desires and needs. That's a good place to look for patterns. You'll be able to spot certain behaviors, actions, or beliefs that define your core Values. Document those patterns - the ones that truly represent your worldview and personality. Odds are, you already know what matters to you; you just haven't framed it as your "Values."

- List Your Positive Moments: Find a cozy spot and jot down the times you felt pure joy, peace, or fulfillment - moments, people, places, situations. Capture the emotions and mental states you experienced.

- Explore Your Dark Side: Don't ignore the negative or shadow side of life. Identify times you felt frustrated, disappointed, or angry. How did you react? What did you learn? This is all part of your journey.

- Take Stock of the Present: Set aside the first two lists and think about who you are right now. Write down five words or phrases that represent your current beliefs and how you want others to see you.

These three angles - your desires from Chapter 7, your high and low experiences, and your current self-image - will show you where your core Values overlap. Write them down in one place. This exercise Is your Core Value Creation process. You're documenting who you are.

Going Deeper

Once you have a draft of your core Values, describe each one in at least 10 bullet points. Explain why each value matters - include situations, actions, and behaviors. You're creating a detailed, personal snapshot of what your Values mean in real life. For example, here's an abbreviated version of my Health value:

- Nutrition over calories: Focus on quality instead of quantity.

- Question health trends: Be open to new ideas, but integrate them with caution.

- Maintain optimal condition: Keep your body strong and your mind at peace.

- Push boundaries carefully: Explore your limits but be responsible.

- Quality in everything: Apply high standards to relationships, sleep, food, etc.

- Embrace fasting: A secret key to longevity - practiced responsibly.

- Be picky with supplements: Don't just blindly follow hype.

- Develop relaxation tools: Techniques for both body and mind.

- No guilt: Reject external pressure or self-blame for pursuing wellness.

- Regular health checks: At least once a year.

- Manage stress: Recognize and recover quickly.

- Allow controlled chaos: Welcome new experiences to mitigate resistance to change.

- Stop when needed: Walk away from unhealthy experiences, including toxic books, perspectives, or relationships.

Sure, these look like guidelines - because that's exactly the point. These are the principles I live by. It may take a while to create a comprehensive list for each of your Values. Take as long as you need.

You're planning to achieve an impossible Vision while executing a challenging Mission, so your Values need to be crystal clear.

Don't try to implement all your Values at once; it can be overwhelming. Focus on one value for at least three months, dedicating an hour a day to practicing or learning about it. With all the notes you've made, you'll have a good sense of the lifestyle changes you need. If your value is Health, it might mean committing to home-cooked meals or short, regular naps. The point is to do it daily. Even after defining your core Values (which could take months or years), you'll likely revisit them every so often to refine or update. It's okay if they evolve.

Values aren't about being perfect. They're about consistency and cutting out the noise that keeps you from designing the life you want. Sometimes it helps to create a Value Statement - a single sentence that sums up your approach, giving others a window into how you operate. It attracts people who share your aspirations or who might help you solve mutual challenges.

A Value Statement is the headline of your life. Make it a habit to review your Values along with your Vision and Mission at least once a year. Life will change, and you should be proactive in adapting your personal framework to reflect new truths. Self-discovery goes hand in hand with self-reflection, which you'll need to implement as a structured practice if you want to keep growing. What mattered yesterday might not matter today, and it almost certainly will shift tomorrow. As you build more Personal Maturity, your Values will deepen or evolve. Keep everything documented. Core Values are the bedrock of personal identity. They represent your beliefs, ideology, philosophy, and mindset in a clean, organized way. They guide tough life decisions, shield you from distractions, and keep you focused on what genuinely matters. And they help shape the personal Qualities you develop - who you become.

With that, let's discover our Qualities.

CHAPTER 9

QUALITIES

> *"Your personal Qualities will determine your success more than any other factor."*
>
> - Brian Tracy

There are many reasons why people enjoy strong friendships, successful business partnerships, healthy family bonds, or even positive interactions with strangers. One core reason is simple: These people accept us for who we are. Our Qualities - the traits we develop through our meaningful experiences - are recognized by others without us having to seek their approval. Some Qualities drive us toward success, while others might hold us back from reaching our Vision.

Qualities are a part of your Life Design. You're still working on understanding who you are, what you want, and, most importantly, what you can accomplish. That's why I want to introduce a few foundational Qualities you can start developing before you refine your own unique set.

Five Foundational Qualities

- Passion: Passion serves as the engine that propels you forward - a powerful love for what you do, your Big Dream, and your Vision. It's what emboldens you to make tough choices in pursuit of your goals. Passion can turn the ordinary into the extraordinary, making work feel joyful and Dream feel attainable. You'll see a clear difference between someone who's truly passionate and someone who just feels obligated. That's not to say everything in life requires passion, but the most crucial parts of your Mission do. It's also a handy way to check if you're on the right path.

- Accountability: Accountability is about taking ownership of outcomes. It reminds you that you are the architect of your life. It's a powerful antidote to the Follower's Mindset, urging you to look inward, learn from mistakes, and continually strive to be better. It's time to assume total accountability for your existence. When you accept "extreme accountability" - even for negative events and challenging people - it can spark profound Transformation. Become the person who takes complete responsibility for your life, actions, and decisions.

- Discipline: Discipline is what keeps you on the path you've chosen. It's the capacity to set goals and stick with them, resisting short-term temptations for long-term rewards. It's a critical factor in nearly every success story, bringing predictability and consistency. Over time, outsiders might think It's easy for you, but in reality, the foundation Is rigorous, disciplined work.

- Consistency: Consistency is the key to steady progress - the act of performing small but meaningful tasks repeatedly until they accumulate into substantial results. It converts disciplined actions into habits and ensures you build on your efforts day after day.

- Open-Mindedness: This is being receptive to new ideas, experiences, and viewpoints. After your first Mission, you'll need to choose a second, and open-mindedness helps you embrace fresh opportunities, new challenges, and unfamiliar territory. It expands your thinking, fuels learning, and allows you to venture beyond your comfort zone. It's essential for innovation and for breaking free from Borrowed Success.

Real-Life Application

You're probably familiar with Fred Rogers, who spent over 50 years creating children's television. Best known as the host of Mister Rogers' Neighborhood, Fred is an iconic figure in the U.S. His Vision was clear yet profound: "To create a positive influence through TV." His Mission centered on providing meaningful, educational programming for children - even though the industry was dominated by fast-paced, sensational shows that often led to the Follower's Mindset and Social Debt. Critics were skeptical, but Fred's Qualities allowed him to succeed.

- He used his passion for helping kids to build content that was both entertaining and emotionally supportive.

- He took accountability for every aspect of his show, ensuring it delivered a positive and inclusive message.

- His discipline showed in the careful planning of each episode - day in and day out - creating a lasting impact for generations.

- Through consistency, he reinforced themes of kindness, acceptance, and understanding, earning trust and loyalty from his audience.

- He stayed open-minded, gathering feedback and adapting as necessary to remain relevant for decades.

Fred Rogers became a powerful example of what happens when Vision, Mission, Values, and Qualities align. He transformed children's TV into a medium for Growth and positivity for millions of kids.

Why Your Qualities Matter

- Increased Confidence: Being aware of - and actively using - your Qualities boosts your confidence, especially when the going gets tough. Recognizing your strengths fortifies your belief in your ability to fulfill your Mission, helping you tackle new challenges with a positive outlook.

- Life Satisfaction: Qualities, actions, and results line up in a way that naturally leads to joy and fulfillment. Acting with self-assurance in pursuit of your Vision and Mission gives life a sense of purpose and meaning, which raises your overall satisfaction. This may well be your first time driving your own Life Success rather than relying on Borrowed Success.

- Leadership Skills: Knowing your Qualities helps you communicate effectively, build relationships, and set clear expectations for others, all while respecting their strengths. You become a leader on a Mission that points toward a bright Vision. Self-awareness can also inspire and motivate those around you, creating a supportive and innovative environment.

Evolving Your Qualities

Like Values, Qualities should be used as frequently as possible - but especially when they're needed most. Qualities can also change over time; self-reflection is vital. Devote at least a little time each year to reviewing and refining them. That's part of being open-minded.

- Journaling: Track your experiences, goals, and emotional states. Gathering data throughout the year helps you see trends and make informed changes.

- Feedback: Seek unfiltered opinions from people you trust (or even relative strangers, in certain contexts). Some might hesitate to be brutally honest, so find ways to encourage genuine input.

- Assessments: Use psychological evaluations or personality tests to gain professional insights. The Big Five Personality Traits Test is a solid starting point.

Your Qualities shape who you are and outline what people can expect from you. They create a predictable framework for your behavior. The five mentioned here (Passion, Accountability, Discipline, Consistency, and Open-Mindedness) should serve as a baseline - a starting point to test yourself as you work on your Mission. You'll uncover more Qualities, or expand on them, as you move closer to your Vision. Reflection and adaptation are key.

By now, you should have a clearer picture of your Vision, Mission, Values, and Qualities. The next question is who you really are at your core and what ideology you identify with.

Let's discuss Identity next.

CHAPTER 10

IDENTITIES

> *"Continuous effort - not strength or intelligence - is the key to unlocking our potential."*
>
> **- Winston Churchill**

Time to look in the mirror.

There's one last piece to complete your Life Design puzzle: Growth Identity. This concept is crucial because, as you advance on your Mission, you'll face increasingly complex scenarios in your life. You need a mechanism that will help you stay competitive - against the world, society, and your own inner pressures. Willpower alone can carry you only so far. Growth Identity offers something more sustainable.

Here are three principles you can use to develop your Growth Identity:

Cut out the Noise: Your self-discovery and reflection journey may have unearthed thoughts, ideas, and desires that had been hiding for years. When I did my Mission exploration exercise, I wrote down over 1,500 things I thought I wanted or needed; I eventually cut it down to fewer than 100. That exercise gave me a sense of full control over my life. Everything else was just noise, and I chose to leave everything that wasn't necessary for my Mission behind. That lifted a massive weight off my mind. For the first time in my life, I knew exactly what I wanted.

View Life as a Metagame: Life is a playing field where you can choose specific areas to master - like an Olympic athlete honing a sport, or an inventor pioneering new technology. Which Values and Qualities you focus on are entirely up to you. Decide what you want to excel at and train accordingly.

Gamify your life: No matter your current level, you can always improve. You must be ready to challenge your own beliefs and commitments. Sometimes you'll feel as though you're regressing, but you're actually leveling up in your Personal Maturity.

Growth Identity is built on these principles, often from the ground up - or by starting over. Age is irrelevant. For instance, I once built an incredibly successful team. I grew it from 2 to 30 people in a year and a half only to watch envious management take it away from me. Overnight, I lost what I believed was my core identity - being a great leader. It sent shockwaves through my entire perception of my professional life and career development. I was physically present in the office but mentally out for 6 months, restarting my engines to take on new challenges and opportunities. I took these invaluable lessons with me, and they all became a part of my Growth Identity.

Why Growth Identity?

Think of the Follower's Mindset as an identity, too. If you aim to live a purposeful life, you will want to replace the Follower's Mindset with Growth Identity. Remember, you're also grappling with Social Debt and Borrowed Success. To break free from these limiting mindsets, you've already:

- Dreamed big to form your Vision

- Defined a Mission that will take you there

- Established Values that guide your decisions

- Identified the Qualities required for success

Now, you need to become the person who can tie it all together by embracing Growth Identity.

Core Ideas of Growth Identity

- Starting From Zero: We begin life with zero knowledge of the world and discover meaning through a mix of pleasant and painful experiences. Our personalities evolve as we grow up, often defaulting to a Follower's Mindset and Social Debt Identity. That's why critical thinking is so important - ideally, your parents taught you this skill. If you didn't get that training, it's your job to do it for yourself now. Growth occurs when you question your beliefs, systems, and surroundings. You'll encounter pushback and risk not fitting in. Yet by analyzing various viewpoints, you become less judgmental and less controlled by former habits. This doesn't mean everyone else is wrong; people are simply at different stages in their Personal Maturity journey - some remain stuck at level one forever. You want to keep evolving so you can become an independent thinker, resistant to toxic gurus and manipulative prophets. Critical thinking is the first step in building a Growth Identity. Once you begin to see the world differently, there's no going back.

- Mastering Communication: One of the most important skills you can develop is communication - speaking, writing, listening, presenting, and thinking. It's your negotiation tool, influence tool, learning tool, invention tool, and creation tool - all rolled into one. Critical thinking plus communication is a powerful combination. Some aspects of your Mission might require public speaking, major negotiations, or inspiring people with your ideas. Strong communication skills also feed into your Growth Identity as you surround yourself with people who are more advanced than you in certain areas. It will help you learn from them and build a network of like-minded individuals who are willing to help you achieve your Vision.

- Caring for Body, Mind, and Spirit: Once you commit to a Growth Identity, you'll realize that body, mind, and spirit are essential pillars for supporting the life you want. You have to prioritize these areas, which is increasingly challenging in modern society. But it's always been difficult - that's the point. You can only advance as far as your health allows. Take care of your physical well-being with nutritious food and exercise; nurture your mind with meaningful experiences and knowledge; tend to your spirit through self-reflection or any practice that keeps you grounded. You deserve to be both healthy and successful.

With critical thinking, communication, and health in place, you'll have a pragmatic lens through which to view the world. You'll likely start filtering out people and habits that don't align with your goals. For example, I once craved attention so much that I built a social circle of people who didn't really care about me unless I contacted them first. I made the tough decision to stop contacting them. Almost no one reached out on their own, so I effectively removed 90% of people from my life - and never regretted it.

As you move toward minimalism - reducing consumption and waste - you may face both internal and external resistance. In 2017, I donated 90% of my clothes. Like many, I was guilty of buying more than I needed. That step sparked a shift toward simplicity (now one of my core Values). At the time, I still worked on Wall Street and ended up with just two dress shirts, one suit, and a few t-shirts and pants. I found it incredibly freeing, and I still keep my wardrobe minimal. The habit of decluttering extends to everything else - removing irrelevant items and focusing on what matters. That's the essence of Growth Identity: a pragmatic approach to thinking and living. Although it may feel daunting at first, it can be surprisingly fun. As Marie Kondo said "To truly cherish the things that are important to you, you must first discard those that have outlived their purpose.

Recognizing Patterns

Growth Identity also revolves around patterns - discovering new ones, refining old ones, and optimizing whatever works. These patterns might be:

- Behavioral: For example, drinking water before meals instead of during, which once aggravated my stomach issues.

- Systemic: Techniques like "One Thing a Day" where you focus on your most important task. Identify your "one thing" and prioritize it above all else (from the book The One Thing), which increases focus and productivity by tackling one significant task daily.

- Process-Oriented: Monthly or annual budgeting to understand your finances and save more effectively.

Patterns appear everywhere, and once you notice them, you'll be in a better position to either harness them or break them. Think of it as a superpower: You see what others overlook, giving you an edge in shaping your life.

Trevor Noah, a famous comedian from South Africa, serves as a great example of Growth Identity in action. He faced racial discrimination, social exclusion, financial hardship, and had few opportunities early on - conditions that could defeat anyone. However, Trevor discovered a passion for comedy, which allowed him to connect with diverse audiences and challenge outdated norms. This passion pushed him toward Growth Identity: He learned to communicate complex cultural and political themes through humor, encouraging open dialogue while he entertained people. He adapted to new environments, from local clubs in Johannesburg to international TV shows. Each time he stepped out of his comfort zone, he sharpened his skills, ultimately becoming a top comedian, TV host, and author - proof that you can scale new heights of Personal Maturity no matter where your journey begins.

Putting Growth Identity into Practice

So, what now? The straightforward answer is to apply these rules daily until they feel natural. The harder truth is that it takes time. You're trying to undo years of Follower's Mindset, Social Debt, and Borrowed Success. Have patience with yourself and move at a sustainable pace. Not everything will click in a neat sequence -

sometimes you'll develop Values or Qualities before solidifying your Mission or Vision. Growth Identity can feel like a rollercoaster. Buckle up; you'll accumulate plenty of meaningful experiences along the way. If you ask yourself what alternatives you have, you likely already know: Stay stuck, or move forward.

You've now identified the elements that help you find Life Purpose. Next, we'll head to the whiteboard and design your life, tying it all together into a simple framework. "Simple" doesn't mean weak - often, the simplest solutions are the most powerful.

Let's do Life Design.

CHAPTER II

LIFE DESIGN

> *"Life isn't about finding yourself. Life is about creating yourself."*
> - George Bernard Shaw

It's time to put all the pieces together.

Here are the Challenges we've outlined so far: Follower's Mindset, Social Debt, and Borrowed Success, which ultimately rob us of our sense of purpose. They leave us dependent on others, and lead us to drift through life unconsciously. Most of us deal with these challenges daily, in one form or another.

Here are the steps we've outlined to free ourselves to find and pursue our Life Purpose:

Step #1 – Life Design: This is a behavioral system made up of Big Dream, Vision, Mission, Values, Qualities, and Growth Identity. Life

Design helps you organize these elements into something that's easy to understand, implement, and apply. Life Design puts you back in control - letting you live intentionally, mitigate challenges, and ultimately find your Life Purpose.

Step #2 – Personal Maturity: This is a framework that helps you effectively apply Life Design principles, measure your progress, and fine-tune your approach. It enables continuous Growth on your path toward your Vision. It's like the strong roots of a tree that help it grow despite the weather (Figure 6).

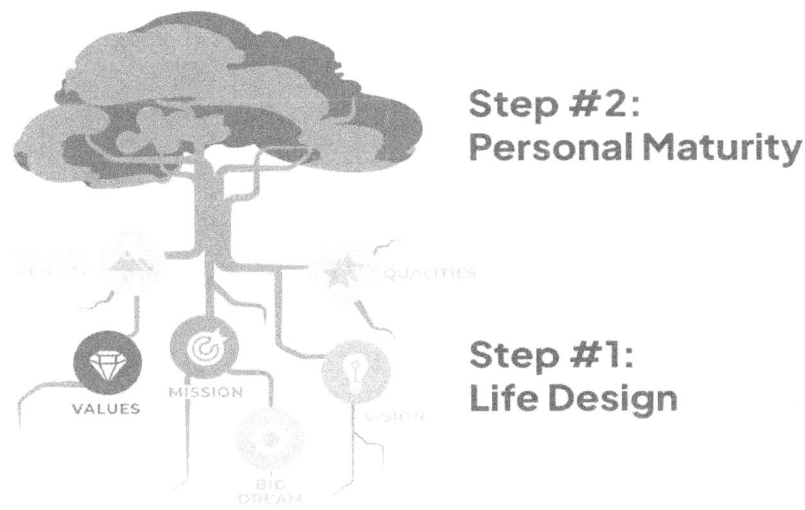

Figure 6. "Step 1 and 2 in finding Life Purpose"

The engine behind Life Design is Self-Discovery - it's how you unearth hidden truths about why, how, and what you truly want. Meanwhile, the driver of Personal Maturity is Self-Reflection - an ongoing assessment process that shows you how to grow and improve. Life Design helps you find your purpose, while Personal Maturity helps you become effective at living it. In Sections 3 and 4, we'll dive deeper into Personal Maturity and best practices that can make you unstoppable.

I suggest drafting your Life Design first, then applying Personal Maturity best practices. But life rarely follows a neat sequence - you might already have some pieces in place. As long as you grasp the big picture and can fill any gaps through Self-Reflection and Self-Discovery, you'll have the strength to overcome almost any challenge (Figure 7).

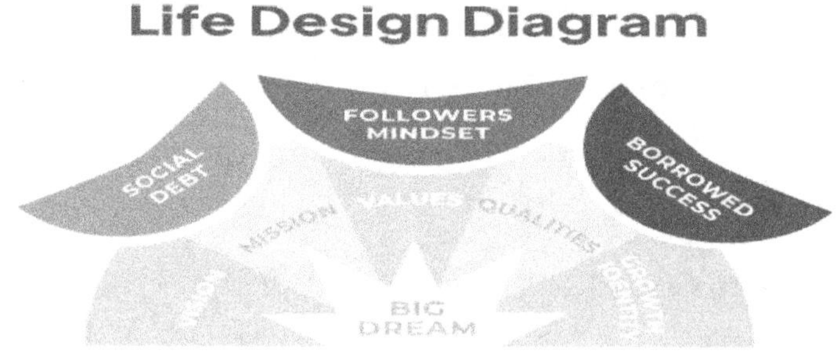

Figure 7. "Three big challenges that Life Design can help to fix"

How the Life Design System Fits Together

- The Big Dream (Why): At the core of everything is your Big Dream - your ego, your North Star. This is the cornerstone of purposeful living. Your Big Dream might be unreachable, but that's the point: you should do everything you can to make it happen. Your Big Dream brings a sense of boundless freedom and eliminates fear or hesitation.

- Vision (How): With your Big Dream in place, you can craft a Vision - your unique path to achieving the impossible. This will showcase your potential greatness and outline how your Dream can change the world. Your Vision also inspires others to join in and help make it real.

- Mission (What): Next, convert that inspiration into one or more Missions - concrete steps or initiatives that move you closer to your Vision. Every Mission, whether it succeeds or fails, tells you if you're on the right track or if you need to pivot. Each Mission should have a written statement and an action plan.

Becoming That Person

Once you know your why, how, and what, the final piece is becoming the person who can pull it off. That's where Values, Qualities, and Growth Identity come in - plus the Personal Maturity framework, which you'll learn more about later.

- Values describe who you are. They guide you through difficult decisions - which you'll definitely face on your Mission. If you truly value something or someone, you'll prioritize it.

- Qualities describe what you're capable of - your key to success. Some Qualities you'll develop through hard work; others might come naturally. Either way, your Qualities will help you close any gaps revealed by your Values so you can tackle your Mission with confidence.

- Growth Identity is the mechanism that empowers you to reach your Vision and carry out your Mission. It ties into Personal Maturity, enabling you to turn the unknown and impossible into tangible outcomes by using your Values and Qualities. It's a Growth-oriented mindset that lets you thrive on challenges - turning "failures" into stepping stones on the way to your Vision.

Putting these elements together forms a cohesive Life Design that drives you toward greatness. You may have each piece documented separately and wonder how it all fits. But when you step back and see the whole picture, you'll spot connections and areas for improvement. That's the beauty of Life Design.

Life Design in Action

Wangari Maathai was a Kenyan environmental and political activist who founded the Green Belt Movement in 1977. Her organization has planted over 51 million trees in Kenya, tackled climate-change issues, and empowered thousands of women with economic opportunities and leadership roles. She was also the first African woman to receive the Nobel Peace Prize.

How did Wangari Maathai achieve so much, despite growing up in a rural setting and facing gender discrimination, political backlash, and social resistance? Let's map out her Life Design:

- Big Dream (Why): Wangari aimed for a sustainable environment that could support future generations - and believed women should lead that cause. She firmly held that environmental conservation and women's rights were key to social progress.

- Vision (How): She envisioned large-scale reforestation efforts driven by women. In her mind, empowering women to be at the forefront of environmental work would strengthen people's livelihoods and ecosystems.

- Mission (What): The Green Belt Movement launched initiatives to get women planting trees, restoring degraded land, and advocating for sustainable development. Their Mission involved running tree-planting campaigns, teaching environmental education, and pushing for policy reforms.

- Values: Maathai's guiding Values included environmental stewardship, women's empowerment, resilience, and social justice - Values that shaped the Green Belt Movement and her broader activism.

- Qualities: She was courageous, determined, compassionate, and a natural leader. Her ability to unite communities around a shared cause carried her through enormous obstacles of divorce, imprisonment, opposition from the government and lots of harassment due the nature of her work.

- Growth Identity: Wangari stayed open to learning and innovation, adjusting her methods as challenges surfaced. Her Growth Mindset propelled her work to new heights over time, expanding the movement's scope.

By weaving all these elements together, Wangari Maathai tackled complex issues, inspired countless individuals, and made a lasting difference.

What Is Life Purpose?

It's the sum total of your Life Design - a way to chase the impossible while claiming full accountability for your existence. Having a Life Purpose means you're in charge, taking on potentially unrealistic goals, and refusing to quit. Don't be surprised if you feel an immediate sense of purpose just by creating your Life Design. It might be the first time you've done something purely for yourself - and that can be incredibly powerful, like crafting an entirely new universe that revolves around you.

Now that you know how your life can be "designed," let's jump into Personal Maturity and learn how to supercharge your Life Purpose.

SECTION 3 - PERSONAL MATURITY

> "It is not the strongest of the species that survives, nor the most intelligent, but the one most responsive to change."
>
> - Charles Darwin

So, after all the self-discovery work you've done - building a Life Design and clarifying your Life Purpose - do you still have more to do? In short: Yes. Reality is complex.

After my separation, I lived alone in a tiny apartment in New York, spending weekends on endless walks through the city. I'd deliberately get lost, hoping to 'bump into' purpose around the next block. It gave me plenty of time to realize how meaningless my life had become, which pushed me toward an even deeper self-discovery.

You live in a world filled with people wrestling with a Follower's Mindset, Social Debt, and Borrowed Success. Moving directly toward your Big Dream can be tough, and with so much pressure surrounding you, it's tempting to give up. Sometimes even your best efforts might not cut it.

What you need is a plan and a mechanism to execute your Dream effectively (as you stay open to the changes you might need to make along the way). That mechanism is Personal Maturity. I want to show you how to break down your Life Design into actionable steps, gauge your progress, and create a systematic method to achieve extraordinary results. Personal Maturity blends elements of psychology, philosophy, self-help, personal Growth, and Transformation. There are countless helpful books in each of these areas, but this book aims to give you the big picture so you can make more informed choices and meaningful changes.

In this section, we'll dive into the fundamentals of Personal Maturity. For now, just remember that it's an execution and improvement system. Ultimately, it's a guide that can help you find answers no matter where you stand in life or how you feel at the moment. Picture it as a snapshot you can keep referring to.

I'll walk you through my version of a Personal Maturity Framework, but I want you to know one thing right from the start: If you truly commit yourself to this path, you'll end up creating a custom approach that fits your life story. My goal is simply to give you a foundation to begin with.

Let's start by looking at a great example of someone who developed his own system, Ray Dalio. You may know him well - he founded Bridgewater Associates, one of the world's largest and most successful hedge funds. His journey was far from linear. In 1982, he lost everything when he bet against the market. That setback forced him to rethink his investing approach and, ultimately, his entire life. In doing so, he built tools that have helped millions. He realized he needed a better way to manage his own behaviors, leading him to apply Radical Transparency and Radical Truth to his personal and professional life. (We'll talk about Radical Philosophy in Chapter 16.) These methods laid the groundwork for a mature, systematic approach that involved:

- Radical Transparency: Dalio fostered a culture of total openness at Bridgewater Associates. By being honest about mistakes - his own and those of his team - he believed everyone could learn and grow together. Achieving this meant adopting a mature mindset to handle criticism and failure constructively.

- Principles: Dalio wrote his own principles covering everything from decision-making to interpersonal relationships. These guidelines formed a consistent framework for navigating complex situations in business and beyond. His book Principles: Life and Work details this journey toward Personal Maturity.

- Learning from Failures: Dalio saw every failure as a chance to gain new insights and refine his strategies. This habit of continuous learning and adaptation is a hallmark of Personal Maturity.

- Measuring Progress: He insisted on objective feedback and data to gauge outcomes, then used that information to make adjustments. This systematic approach kept him aligned with his long-range Vision.

- Balancing Reality and Goals: Dalio was bluntly honest about present realities while still pursuing his goals. For him, Personal Maturity was about accepting the facts of a situation yet striving to make it better.

By now, it's probably clear: Personal Maturity is all about taking a systematic approach to your life, seeing the big picture, crafting a plan, taking action, and fine-tuning everything along the way. You need a system like this to carry out your Life Design - so that it becomes more than just scribbles in a notebook. Take my system, adapt and refine it, and build your own unique version to unlock your greatest potential.

Let's start by looking more closely at what Personal Maturity really is.

CHAPTER 12

PERSONAL MATURITY 101

> *"Maturity is the capacity to endure uncertainty."*
> - John Huston Finley

What's the most boring way to start a chapter? Right - definitions.

But here's one you need: Personal Maturity is a meta-state. You're always operating at a certain level of the Personal Maturity scale, and that level might - or might not - be enough to achieve your Life Purpose. That means you need a series of personal Transformations to move from one level to another. This is why I call it the Personal Maturity Journey: You'll go up and down as you make personal, social, financial, mental, spiritual, and other changes that help you evolve. These changes vary in complexity, and I actually suggest simple changes so your body and mind can adapt. It's even smaller than the "1% rule" idea. If that resonates, you're on the right track.

Mentally, the Personal Maturity Journey is a cycle of self-reflection and self-discovery that helps you understand exactly where you are on the Personal Maturity scale and figure out how to grow so you can better implement your Life Design.

Personal Maturity is you - the current version of yourself, a snapshot of who you are right now. When you learn to measure your Personal Maturity, you'll see positive progress trends year over year. Unsurprisingly, these will be the areas you invest the most effort into improving. Sometimes you'll notice that by changing certain parts of your life, you stop worrying about or caring for specific things. That can be a major breakthrough - letting you safely move on and find peace. Expect peaks and valleys along the way - that's part of the design.

To help you on this journey, I'll share the Personal Maturity Framework, which groups critical elements of life - some you already know from Section 2. The first category is Life Design, covering Vision, Mission, Values, Qualities, and Growth Identity. If you followed Section 2, you've already built a Life Design, probably without even realizing it was part of Personal Maturity. Now, we'll measure, understand, and enhance that design through a leveling system we'll discuss soon.

Along with Life Design, the Personal Maturity Framework has categories for Social Success, Personal Efficiency, and Transformation, combining a total of 24 elements. Each element represents some aspect of you and your life.

Each element in the Personal Maturity Framework can be measured on a scale from 0 to 5, where:

- 0 means chaos or that the element is completely missing,
- 5 means total mastery - potentially on a global level.

When you average your maturity across all elements, you get your Personal Maturity Level - this process is called a Maturity Assessment. It's essentially a self-assessment using a straightforward rating system, but you have to be brutally honest about it. In my experience from mentoring others, most people land between 1.7 and 2.6, which isn't bad. If you're below 1.5, it's a concern, and if you're 3.5 or above, you're in a position to help others elevate their maturity. Hitting 5.0 on every element is almost impossible because life keeps changing - but it's a helpful aspirational target. In Chapter 13, I'll show you how to assess your current score.

The most natural way to boost Personal Maturity is to create a Life Design (Section 2) and then complete a Mission full of meaningful experiences. Those experiences convert into knowledge and wisdom, which gradually pushes up your Personal Maturity Level - more is better. Once your Life Design is rolling, I generally suggest picking a few elements of the Personal Maturity Framework and focusing on them for at least six months. Your progress should be noticeable to others before you move on to another set of elements.

Early in 2023, I decided to redefine my professional life and embarked on a Mission to consult for startups. I'd noticed too many promising companies failing for avoidable reasons, and I felt an urge to do something about it - butI wasn't sure how. I had just left my VP role at WorkFusion and begun leading a team of Technical Program Managers at Twitter, optimizing infrastructure costs. Looking back, my career path seemed linear, yet it never really was - it often felt chaotic. I also realized I'd done so many different things that I had a wealth of knowledge sitting idle in my head.

I had doubts, of course, but I jumped in and started consulting on the side. I networked, asked for referrals, did tons of research, and took notes on my insights, and I soon found myself advising multiple tech startups at various stages, calling myself a "professional consultant."

At first, it felt great to see my knowledge help one company increase user engagement and another become more efficient. But the more I worked, the more it felt like just another job - I'd charge an hourly rate, but never truly solve problems at the root. I built a bit of a reputation, but after nine months and several projects, it dawned on me that this wasn't the right Mission for me. Instead of "fixing" startups one at a time, I realized I should teach them how to fix themselves, so they wouldn't need consultants like me.

So I founded The Startup Academy, inspired by the belief that the world deserves more successful companies - organizations that can truly make a difference. I sat in front of a camera and began recording educational videos on every topic a startup might need: strategy, organizational structure, avoiding early-stage pitfalls. I also reached out to CEOs globally, inviting them to interviews so I could share their knowledge too, all on my YouTube channel. At one point, I worried I'd become just another online influencer chasing likes and views. But I reminded myself that my Mission was to offer practical knowledge for free, not entertain people for vanity metrics.

Initially, hardly anyone paid attention - no surprise, since I'm not a celebrity. But I pressed on because my goal was to help more people. Over time, I got invitations to speak at internal workshops and private communities on topics that ranged from scaling a business to leadership. It stayed a hobby, but a fun and meaningful one. Right now, The Startup Academy is on yet another Mission: to create the best possible knowledge hub for startups - offering lectures, interviews, articles, master classes, and courses. It's a bumpy ride, mainly due to competition and my own learning curve. But that's part of the process: I'm learning as much as I teach others.

I share this story to show how your Personal Maturity Journey evolves along with your focus. You need time to explore, research, adapt, and become something different, if necessary. Start with the smallest milestone, try it, then repeat and adjust. Each meaningful experience deepens your maturity in a specific area, letting you decide whether to persist or pivot.

Tying It All Together

There's a correlation between advancing toward your Life Purpose and achieving a higher Personal Maturity Level. If you crave more control over your life, I strongly suggest measuring your maturity at least once a year (Figure 8). It can seamlessly fit into whatever reflective practices you already use, adding structure and clarity. It may even solve some of the puzzles you've been wrestling with.

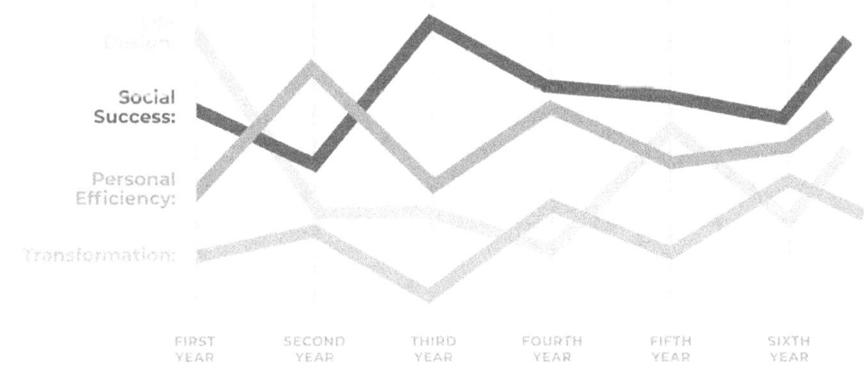

Figure 8. "Personal Maturity trend changes over years"

The Personal Maturity Journey is both profound and rewarding. It's limitless, full of the opportunities you create through meaningful experiences. Of course, it's not easy but this book aims to give you the tools and enough confidence to act. You'll embark on intense self-reflection to examine your beliefs, understand the world, and chase the impossible.

Personal Maturity is the philosophical guide to becoming a new version of you. Life Design is your destination; Personal Maturity is your map.

Let's explore the Personal Maturity Framework in more detail.

CHAPTER 13

PERSONAL MATURITY FRAMEWORK

> *"Growth is the only evidence of life."*
> - John Henry Newman

What Is Your Personal Maturity Level?

It all begins with the idea that personality development should have a logical blueprint. Sure, there are countless psychological tests offering personality summaries, but in creating one that would work for me, I wanted to add gamification - a leveling and trait mapping system that has grown into the Personal Maturity Framework. By combining all the necessary elements, creating assessment questions, and building a grading scale, this framework has evolved into a systematic approach. It incorporates all the research and documentation I've compiled, charting the differences between levels to help you track your progress.

The Personal Maturity Framework is, at its core, a set of life elements grouped into categories and broken down by distinct levels. It's a self-evolving mechanism: the more you invest in Personal Maturity, the more you'll see that you can create your own version. My aim here is to give you a starting framework. As you gain confidence, you'll adapt and optimize it to suit your needs. Understanding how systems operate is crucial if you want to master them. Data-driven decision-making about life can be a lot of fun.

The Personal Maturity Framework has four categories with 24 elements (Figure 9) in total.

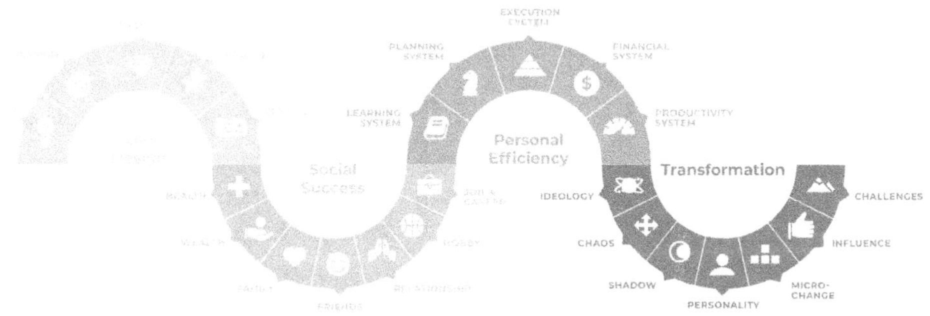

Figure 9. "Categories and Elements of Personal Maturity Framework"

Each element is a facet of life that influences us in unique ways. People with a low Personal Maturity Level typically show big imbalances among these elements and categories. That's why I always recommend starting with Life Design - you need to be clear on what you want before you invest in elements that matter. Often, people spend time in areas that don't really push them closer to their true goals. It's also worth noting that reaching the highest level across all 24 elements is extremely challenging - unless you aim to be the first to do so!

The Categories in Brief

- Life Design: We've covered this in Section 2. You'll set unrealistically big goals - why not? You're in control, and even if it seems impossible, you owe it to yourself to try. Life Design is about laying out the foundation and structure for achieving your purpose.

- Social Success: This category covers areas you've likely thought about since childhood: Health, Wealth, Family, Friends, Relationships, Hobbies, and Career. Many people who feel aimless in life excel here because they've been taught these areas are all that matter. But Social Success also acts as a wake-up call for those with social challenges or heavy Social Debt. It reveals the sacrifices required for higher Personal Maturity.

- Personal Efficiency: To succeed with your ambitions, you need a systemic approach. You're only as strong as the systems you rely on. I've identified five that can make a major impact:

    - Learning System: Turning knowledge into wisdom

    - Planning System: Structuring your life

    - Execution System: Prioritizing tasks and making solid decisions

    - Financial System: Achieving abundance and staying focused on the Big Dream

    - Productivity System: Operating at your full potential

- Transformation: This is where true personal development happens. It includes deeper psychological and philosophical concepts like Ideology, Chaos, Shadow, Personality, Micro-Change, Influence, and Challenges. We'll explore these in Section 4. This category shows your capacity to adapt, evolve, and transcend who you are. By working on these elements, you become someone new.

The Levels of Personal Maturity

There are six levels in this framework:

- Level 0 – Chaos: A state of confusion and disarray, where you feel lost and unmotivated. You might lack basic knowledge about the element in question - say, finances (and find your money situation in total ruin). Recognizing and accepting you're at Level 0 is the first step toward resolving chaos.

- Level 1 – Awareness: You see the need for change but still feel overwhelmed and unfocused. You know you should improve but are easily distracted. The best move here is to absorb knowledge - read books, attend events, talk to experts or mentors, and figure out a plan. Moving from Level 0 to 1 is an awakening; you realize you must address certain issues to grow.

- Level 2 – Understanding: This is about active practice and learning through trial and error. You might feel a budding sense of what's right vs. wrong. You experiment with new behaviors and strategies to pinpoint the root causes of problems. It's a stage of learning by doing.

- Level 3 – Competence: You can now successfully apply the skills and knowledge you've acquired. You're productive, organized, and have systems in place to handle Life disruptions. It's where critical thinking begins to flourish. You're finally in control and can see what life should look like.

- Level 4 – Excellence: Personal Maturity becomes your second nature. You tackle challenges with ease, no external motivation needed. Your new behaviors have become deeply ingrained habits. You don't just improve; you sustain those improvements.

- Level 5 – Mentorship: This represents absolute freedom - you can positively influence both your own life and the lives of those around you. You may even have a global impact. It's the height of personal Transformation, where giving back your wisdom is the most natural thing in the world. Level 5 doesn't guarantee you'll fulfill your Life Purpose or become "the first" at something, but it enormously boosts your odds.

As you climb these levels, you'll build confidence and decide which elements deserve your attention. That's real control - the power to sacrifice certain elements if you so choose. It might look crazy to outsiders, but you know exactly what you're doing.

Making Your Assessment

You'll assign a maturity level (0 to 5) for each of the 24 elements based on how they currently look in your life. I'll provide more detailed descriptions of each level and element in Appendix A, which you can reference as you do your self-assessment. Keep in mind this framework isn't backed by formal academic research - it's grounded in common sense, practical experience, and personal insights. Feel free to tweak it to fit your reality.

A strong financial system is vital for general life satisfaction and long-term goals. It can liberate you from money worries and fuel your bigger Mission. I like to think my own Financial System is solid, though I'm not a billionaire - just a once-clueless kid from Ukraine who's done okay. Here's what each level of the financial systems says:

- Level 0: Overwhelmed by debt, no real financial knowledge, money in total disarray.

- Level 1: Starting to address instability, consuming resources to learn the basics of money management.

- Level 2: Grasping the need for a personal financial plan, beginning to stabilize income, maybe grow capital.

- Level 3: Financially stable, optimizing strategies, investing, or building long-term wealth.

- Level 4: High financial expertise, possibly recognized as a leader in finance, with consistent success.

- Level 5: Personal financial system so robust it provides total economic freedom and helps others do the same.

I carry some debt, but mostly "good debt" from investments. I don't max out my credit cards. I keep an annual budget plan, do monthly reviews, track overspending, and correct bad habits quickly. I invest faithfully (stocks, crypto, etc.) - it's part of my budget. I know my net worth, how it breaks down, and have seen a 25% year-over-year increase for 12 years running. I used to be financially unstable. I remember one day having $1,600 in my account - enough to scare me into building a real system. Around 2012, when I made just $200 a month in Ukraine, I aimed to earn my first million dollars. Now, I'm beyond that figure, which I've built slowly and steadily. Earning more than $150K a year by 2018, I reached a comfort threshold; more income didn't feel noticeably different, so I switched to maximizing wealth instead of just chasing a higher salary. Based on all this, I'd put myself around Level 3.5.

That's how you do it. If you go through all 24 elements, you'll have a maturity level for each (Figure 10). Then you can average them by category and come up with your overall score. It might seem daunting, but nobody knows you better than you do. Usually, it takes a minute or less per element to compare your reality with the framework descriptions.

My overall maturity in 2023 was 3.2, up from 2.5 in 2022:

- Life Design: 3.3 (was 3.0)

- Social Success: 2.0 (was 1.5)

- Personal Efficiency: 4.2 (was 3.2)

- Transformation: 3.5 (was 2.4)

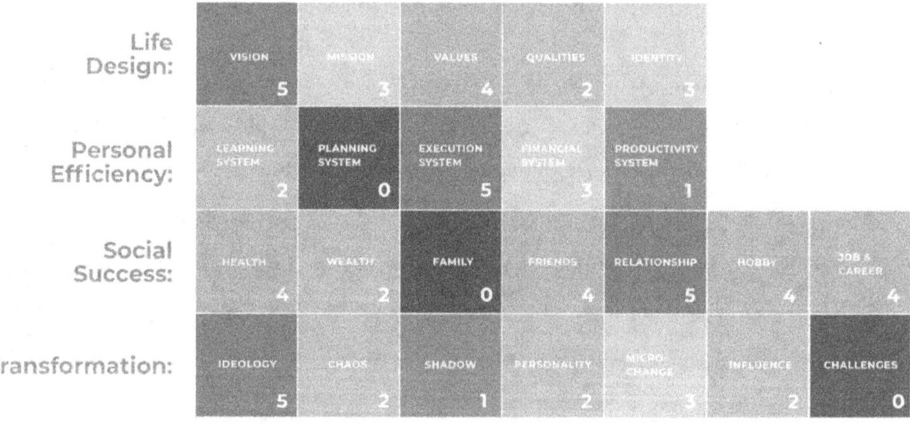

Figure 10. "Assessment results across 24 elements"

You can really see where I invested my energy. In 2024, I'm aiming for near 4.0, but I'm still far from perfect - even though I literally created this system and wrote a book about it. If that doesn't motivate you to start, I'm not sure what will! (Kidding, of course.)

The Benefits of a Personal Maturity Framework

Once you've done this quick assessment and know your Personal Maturity Level, you'll reap several rewards:

- Clarity: You'll have a data-driven way to tackle character development and understand precisely where you stand and where you need to go.

- Accountability: Ultimately, this is on you. You can blame external factors all you want, but once you know the framework, you realize you're in control.

- Motivation: Tracking tangible progress can be hugely motivational. When you see your improvements in real numbers, it encourages you to keep pushing forward.

- Blind Spots: You don't know what you don't know - until now. A holistic view of your life uncovers gaps, prompting you to focus next on what truly matters.

- Personalization: You can customize your development path. Combine elements uniquely. What if you worked on both Shadow and Vision at the same time? Everyone's different, and the framework respects that.

One key point: Personal Maturity isn't a competition - everyone advances at their own pace. The framework exists to support you, not to stress you out.

This framework is designed to help you:

- Overcome the Follower's Mindset, Social Debt, and Borrowed Success.

- Find Life Purpose by building a strong, stable Life Design.

- Develop your character to tackle meaningful Mission effectively.

- Use a structured response system to optimize Growth and foster Transformation.

There are just a few more steps to cover about Personal Maturity: How to integrate it with other personal Growth concepts and apply it in real life.

But first, let's do a Reality Check.

CHAPTER 14

REALITY CHECK

> *"Your time is limited, so don't waste it living someone else's life. Have the courage to follow your heart and intuition."*
>
> **– Steve Jobs**

We humans love when things get better.

You've discovered two major solutions to your existential challenges - Life Design and Personal Maturity - which is already a huge accomplishment. Before we move into the next section on tactics and best practices, I want to lay down a bit of philosophical groundwork for the personal ideology you'll ultimately form. This matters because many people lean on established ideologies like Stoicism, Nihilism, or Existentialism. Nothing wrong with that, but I've observed that building your own personal ideology is often the most logical way to live a truly meaningful life. Some might call it "disobedience" or "disagreement." I call it taking accountability for your existence.

I'm guessing that before you picked up this book, you were sure about at least one thing: Getting more of everything is appealing. More money, time, energy, motivation, positive emotions, knowledge, wisdom, health - the list goes on and on. Culture often teaches us to keep improving, whether physically, emotionally, or spiritually. But you can fall into a trap - especially if you become overly fixated on the material concerns. You might start feeling like you never have enough.

And there's a second, equally demanding culture: personal development. If you're not constantly optimizing yourself, you're "falling behind," or so they say. While I like self-improvement (it's literally what this book is about!), it can become an endless treadmill - an "improvement for improvement's sake" sort of rat race. Because of globalization, social media, and rapid innovation, people get overwhelmed, anxious, depressed, or adopt harmful habits. Recall the Follower's Mindset, Social Debt, and Borrowed Success - they're all part of the same issue: Doing things just to keep up, which leads to a hollow existence. We're here to change that, and you already have Life Design plus Personal Maturity to guide you toward a more meaningful path.

Our goal is simple: Find a way to live a meaningful life.

A Mindset for a Meaningful Life

If you've followed previous chapters, you've seen that much of the work begins with a mindset shift. It can occur naturally through Self-Discovery (Section 2) and Self-Reflection (Section 3). Forcing it prematurely often triggers internal resistance - especially if you haven't tackled your Shadow Work yet (we'll discuss that soon).

However, by doing the Section 2 exercises, you've already made key, irreversible changes. Here's how to amplify them:

- Cultivate Learning: Make learning a habit. Stay curious about life. Check out other people's knowledge - you'll find wisdom in unexpected places. You can start slowly and eventually build a learning system. Maybe focus on up to five influential figures at a time - study them deeply, then move on to new subjects.

- Practice Self-Reflection: Developing Personal Maturity hinges on self-reflection - evaluating your current position, charting your progress, and visualizing where you need to go. Regularly reflecting on your journey transforms how you tackle challenges; you'll start seeing each one as a learning opportunity instead of a roadblock.

- Seek Influence: Surround yourself with people who nurture your Growth. Find a mentor or a psychologist. Or set up a feedback loop with someone who's willing to give you honest input. Remember, you operate in three zones:

  - What you think you know about yourself,

  - What you think others know about you,

  - What people you trust really think and see about you (things you may be blind to).

- Growth often occurs when we discover and embrace that third zone.

Mindset is your first pillar of success in the Personal Maturity journey. You don't need it to be fully formed to start - just be willing to learn and keep an open mind.

Are Your Habits Helping or Hurting?

Real change requires consistent effort. You need habits to keep you on track. Plenty of resources highlight the power of habit formation, and you probably know many of them already. We all have habits - good or bad - that shape our daily routines and, consequently, our lives.

Which habits to build depends on your Life Purpose. You don't have to follow everyone's recommendations - this isn't about fitting in. But obviously, you need non-destructive habits to grow meaningfully. Here are some tips:

- Just Start: Experiment with various new habits. You'll sense almost immediately if a habit "clicks" or not. Try something for 30 days; if it doesn't stick, no big deal. Some believe you must push yourself for 6 months to embed a habit, but I've found that if a habit is right for me, it fits in almost seamlessly.

- Start Small: Changing too many things at once leads to burnout and frustration. Minor changes can yield big benefits. For instance, if you want to start running but find it daunting, begin by simply setting out your running clothes. Next day, maybe put them on. After that, step outside for a minute. Micro-changes often snowball into real progress.

- Be Consistent: Your only job is to show up. If you miss a day or two, don't beat yourself up - just jump back in. You may give up multiple times before a habit finally settles in, and that's okay.

Habits form the second pillar of success. You might not know which ones you need right away, but accept that good habits are essential. Start experimenting.

Ask yourself: How many times are you willing to fail?

Normalizing Failure

Failure can be a powerful teacher, sometimes referred to as a "learning opportunity." But there's a deeper question: When we fail, do we remain the same person, or do we become someone else to succeed next time?

Many people unconsciously choose to stay the same and keep failing at the same level. By embracing mindset changes and robust habits, you can become the person who extracts the full value of each failure. Try these strategies:

- Take Responsibility: There's no one to blame - nor is there any real need for blame. You produced a result (call it "failure" or whatever you like), so own it. Then decide how to move forward.

- Get Feedback: Don't let ego stop you from seeking help. If self-reliance isn't one of your core Values, ask for outside perspectives. They might reveal crucial blind spots faster than you can alone.

Failure is inevitable, but learning to fail is the third pillar of success. Once you accept failure like you accept sleep - as normal - you'll evolve faster.

How Long Can You Pay Attention?

You might need mindfulness - either passive (meditation) or active (journaling) - to stay present. Distractions are everywhere, but focusing on one thing is crucial for self-discovery and self-reflection.

Mindfulness helps you track your thoughts, emotions, and sensations, gaining better insight into your experiences.

- Practice: For many, the first helpful habit is meditation or journaling. Choose whatever feels more natural. Mission will demand laser focus, and mindfulness is how you'll cultivate it.

- Promote: Mindfulness isn't limited to a specific time or place. You can integrate it into everyday moments - paying close attention to how you feel, what you think, or what's happening around you.

Being present and paying attention is the fourth pillar of success in Personal Maturity. This is your Life Purpose on the line - you want to be there for every part of it.

Can You Handle the Heat?

Not everyone will applaud your Vision, Mission, or goals. Some won't understand; they might ridicule or judge you, adding more Social Debt for you to handle. You need resilience - the capacity to recover from difficulties.

If you're already embracing failure, you're on the right track. Real-world experiences, especially those involving social interactions, can test everything you believe in. Here's how to strengthen resilience:

- Practice Self-Care: Worry only about what you can control. Invest your time and energy Into your well-being - physically, mentally, spiritually. Everything else is just input you may or may not use.

- Balance: Resilience develops through successes (building confidence) and failures (building knowledge). It's about navigating between those two. Celebrate your wins, absorb losses, and move on.

Resilience is the fifth pillar of success. Riding the Personal Maturity rollercoaster means you'll eventually become unafraid of change, failure, or the unknown. You'll be unstoppable.

Taking Full Accountability

Once you start integrating these pillars, you'll see it really is all on you - your actions, choices, and path. Why not embrace that completely? After all, this is your Life Design and your Life Purpose at stake. Accountability means committing to your Vision no matter the obstacles. Consider these points:

- Honesty: Be truthful about your progress. Own your outcomes, and if something doesn't work, be willing to pivot. Mindset shifts will support you - everything we've covered works together.

- Measure Progress: Keep records. Are you getting closer to your Vision and Mission, or are you stuck? If so, do you need a new tactic? Without some form of tracking, you won't know.

Accountability is the final pillar in Personal Maturity success. You'll struggle to realize your Life Design or purpose without taking genuine ownership of your decisions.

Stepping Into Reality

Personal Maturity is relatively simple in theory but tough in practice. It offers tools to achieve greatness, provided you tap into your full potential. Some people may lack motivation; others might feel overwhelmed; some may face external roadblocks like resource shortages or unsupportive environments. Something will always try to hold you back - that's why knowing your own ideology (formed by the pillars we've just discussed) is so important.

- Mindset: You need a flexible, open approach to keep evolving.

- Habits: They foster steady progress.

- Failure: Accept it as normal and always learn from it.

- Focus (Mindfulness): Stay present and attentive to each step.

- Resilience: Keep bouncing back, no matter the setbacks.

- Accountability: Recognize you're in charge - no one else.

Life is fluid and changes as you do. Each new level of Personal Maturity reveals a different reality. You may find that tactics that worked at one stage no longer apply in the next. My job is to share strategies so you can adapt, which leads us to the Transformation category of the Personal Maturity Framework. Let's explore how to maximize your Life Design, Social Success, and Personal Efficiency through deeper Transformation.

SECTION 4 - TRANSFORMATION

A lot of people want you to improve - just not beyond their own level.

We often learn too late that when it comes to Life Purpose, you can really only count on yourself. Who else can define your purpose? At best, other people share their wisdom in the form of systems, tactics, or strategies, which you can then translate into knowledge that works for you. That's exactly what I'm going to do in this section.

I'll dive deep into everything related to Transformation, so you can maximize the impact of Personal Maturity in your own life. In Chapter

14 we discussed how you're operating in a complex world that demands a more systematic, structured approach to success. Some of the topics here will be more psychological, others more philosophical, and a few will just be my personal observations. Whatever the case, our focus will be on using your resources - time, energy, skills, and capabilities - to their fullest. We'll explore ways to overcome various challenges and to build a life worth living. We'll also broaden our understanding of personality development, explore our limits, and learn how to break through old dogmas - a deeply rewarding process for character Transformation.

By now, you should have a solid grasp of the core problems the world throws at you - things like the Follower's Mindset, Social Debt, and Borrowed Success - and recognize how they can feed into feeling like you've lost your Life Purpose. That's why we examined Life Design and how to approach recovery in a holistic way. We also learned that Life Design is one of four major categories in the bigger concept called Personal Maturity, along with Social Success, Personal Efficiency, and Transformation. It's time to devote energy to these categories in greater detail and uncover some best practices.

Feel free to adapt and refine the Personal Maturity Framework to fit your own circumstances. This is further proof that I can't dictate your Life Purpose, but I can show you how to discover it. It's up to you whether you follow the advice or let it pass you by.

Now, off to the races. Let's begin with Chaos.

CHAPTER 15

CHAOS

> *"Efficiency is doing better than what is already being done. But true Transformation is about creating systems that make even the impossible attainable."*
> **– Peter Drucker**

Chances are, before starting this book, your life felt chaotic. Even as you read and complete the practical assignments - develop your Life Design and learn about Personal Maturity - you'll still have moments when chaos overwhelms you. Old habits, the people around you, nature, and other external factors all play a big role in your ability to maintain stability. It's natural to experience chaos sometimes, but it's not okay if you can't eventually restore order. To keep growing in Personal Maturity, you need to activate the Personal Efficiency card.

Personal Efficiency is a set of systems designed to help you maximize your Life outcomes - whether you're working on a difficult Mission, practicing Self-Reflection, going through Self-Discovery, or handling daily tasks. "Maximize" is an overused term, so let's say you shouldn't waste your opportunities due to silly mistakes or lack of structure. You want to stay in control and use your time wisely. Allow chaos to appear (as it can be useful), but be ready to tame it. Personal Efficiency is part of Personal Maturity where you make consistent progress toward your Big Dream, accepting that perfection is out of reach but order is not. You anticipate potential obstacles by building systems that keep you moving. Motivation alone won't cut it - structure and discipline are what eat motivation for breakfast.

Why Personal Efficiency?

The most obvious benefit is that you can do more. Less obvious is that you'll also produce higher-quality outcomes. You can move at a slower pace and still accomplish more than you did before. An important note is to avoid comparing yourself with others - progress isn't always visible right away. It often shows up as a calmer mind, sharper focus, healthier reactions to unusual events, less stress, and a sense of emotional balance. Once you've stabilized, you'll see your real productivity and potential, leading you to think about Transformation, another category of Personal Maturity. First, you stabilize your current environment and learn to be effective in it; then, you grow.

Eventually, you'll wake up as a different person.

This journey isn't linear. It's more like an evolution. That's why you must stay committed, even if you don't see quick, measurable results. Life can quickly let you down, prompting you to jump to negative conclusions - but we're going to learn a new way of doing things.

How do we emerge from chaos and build order? I got a crash course in chaos when I worked at Twitter and Elon Musk bought a company. I had 12 months of the most intense experience of my professional life, nothing after that has felt as difficult. Everything moved at breakneck speed with no margin for error. I tested my limits and figured out that a structured and systemic approach can break any chaotic environment. I was able to prove that efficiency isn't about working harder; it's about controlling the seemingly uncontrollable through well-designed systems. You start small, then build and layer on top, little by little. It is that simple.

Cal Newport transformed himself from a distracted undergrad into a celebrated author, computer science professor, and expert on deep work, digital minimalism, efficiency, and productivity. How did he do that?

His academic and professional life were grueling. Cal was juggling teaching, research, writing books, endless emails, meetings, and digital distractions - all while trying to have a personal life. It's nearly impossible to produce high-quality work, let alone live with purpose, under such strain. So, during his PhD at MIT, he decided something had to change. He started experimenting with strategies to increase productivity and minimize distractions, ultimately creating systems for achieving his goals.

A Learning System: Cal set aside specific blocks of time each day for "deep work," allowing him to absorb new information - reading, research, writing - without interruption.

Why a Learning System? From Chapter 14's "Reality Check," you know that mindset change is hard, especially when you don't see the immediate benefits. The best way to start shifting your mind is to learn from others. When you talk, you often just repeat what you already know. But listening invites new knowledge. True, learning can be boring if you're stubborn. That's why you create a learning system that suits your personality. It might involve dedicating one hour a day to different topics, or maybe you do certain kinds of learning on specific days - like Tuesday is reading day, Wednesday is for videos, Thursday is for interviews with experts. Consistency and structure are the keys. And over time, if something stops working, you adapt. Many people give up when their system stops delivering results, but that's the perfect moment to update it. As you keep learning, you'll slowly become a different person, which makes adjusting your system normal.

Core Values of Excellence and Integrity: Cal constantly weighs his commitments and opportunities against his long-term ambitions and Values. He built a priority-making system based on personal principles to reduce noise and distractions.

Why a Priority System? Patterns abound. After you've read 50 business books, you'll recognize many overlapping ideas. It all starts feeling more predictable. You might then establish 7–10 principles to handle 80% of your decisions. That's why you need a learning system first so you can glean insights and craft a priority-making system. It's not about speed - it's about confidence in your choices. A purposeful life will test you with big, tough decisions. You don't need to be an expert in everything, but you do need principles to stay stress-free. These principles should align with your core Values. Patterns and principles also apply to people, helping you spot fakes or opportunists more quickly. Essentially, your priority system blends your Values with a mechanical way of deciding. Maybe you write everything down before acting, or maybe you prefer to wing it. As long as you take responsibility for the outcome, it's okay. And if your system stops working, tweak it again.

Time-Blocking: Cal meticulously schedules his day, week, and month, assigning each task to a specific window. This ensures that he allots enough time for deep work, meetings, and his personal life - a balanced, productive existence.

Why a Planning System? One common path to disappointment is hoping you'll do something but never planning - and thus never doing it. Another is planning but never executing. So a key element of your planning system is the ability to implement. If you don't have this ability, it might mean your system is too weak - which could cause you to slip. Some people plan their entire year in detail; others prefer spontaneity. Which approach yields more in the long run? Start small with the Mission from Section 2. You've already been asked to plan numerous things over a long timeline and then live them out. That's your first planning system. Refine it if you need to. I usually suggest planning to do one important thing a day that moves you toward your Vision. That's 365 steps a year. If you're unsure how to begin, schedule a weekly planning session to define your seven daily tasks - mini steps that fit your real life. Once you can do that, expand to monthly goals and so on. Some people scale it up to annual or even decade-long Vision. There's no single right way; you just need a process that anchors you after life inevitably knocks you off course. Planning is easy; execution is tricky. But by taking small steps, you can be unstoppable.

Cal Newport didn't intentionally build another "system" specifically, but his approach naturally led him to achieve professional success including multiple bestsellers like Deep Work and Digital Minimalism, which have influenced millions. If you also care about the financial side, consider adding a fourth system.

Why a Financial System? Most people's Life Design will involve expenses - maybe big ones. That doesn't mean reckless spending. If your Mission is to cure a disease, you'll invest heavily in research, trials, and experiments - costing months, even years, and a fortune before anything real emerges. You could land funding from investors, but that's never guaranteed. A good cause often comes with a price tag. Thankfully, you don't need all the money upfront. You just need a financial system that moves you forward. Some may go all-in for a big cause; others might keep a steady job and work on their Dream "in the garage" after hours. Both options require a financial plan. You learned from your learning system that you can create something custom as long as it meets your ambitions. For instance, you might want to raise your income each year. Even if it's just a little, beating inflation is a good baseline. Of course, saving helps, but not at the cost of living well - unless it's absolutely essential. Saving without purpose is also a waste; money should enable you to advance your goals. You might invest in your learning, build passive income to focus on your Vision, or directly channel funds into your Mission. Your financial system should outline these habits, mindsets, and events - monthly investment and budgeting, yearly reviews, etc. Decide what's more important: raising your net worth or ROI? Master the basics, then gradually use your resources for significant experiences. Just remember - don't let money become your Life Purpose.

Personal Efficiency stands up to chaos, and Cal Newport is living proof. You can build any system you want, but I'd recommend starting with at least four: Learning System, Planning System, Priority System and Financial System. They'll merge into a broader Productivity System, encompassing all your custom-built processes. Even if you never define your Life Purpose, skip Life Design, and ignore Personal Maturity, these systems alone will elevate your life. You'll keep learning, converting others' wisdom into personal knowledge. You'll grow your wealth and gain financial freedom, make empowered decisions, and shape your existence to experience more satisfaction and less uncertainty.

I hope you aim for an efficient mindset similar to (or surpassing) Cal Newport's. From here, we move forward. Let's keep building and refining your Personal Efficiency - and eventually, we will tackle Transformation head-on.

CHAPTER 16

RADICAL PHILOSOPHY

> *"I never lose. I either win or learn."*
> **– Nelson Mandela**

Michael Phelps is the most decorated Olympian of all time. Ray Dalio stands as one of the most influential finance experts of the 21st century. Elon Musk wields global impact on technology and innovation. What do they all share? The greatest achievements often belong to those with a radical mindset.

Embracing Radicality

Isn't "radical" bad for us? It can be - like poison. In large doses, poison kills; in small, it can heal. People generally dislike anything radical because It lives at the extremes, while society prefers "safe" and "normal." But true greatness rarely springs from the normal;

by definition, "great" isn't average. The fastest, riskiest path to greatness involves a radical philosophy.

Since we're talking about Personal Maturity and Life Purpose, the intensity of radicality you'll need varies according to the size of your Dream. You can learn about it now and apply it thoughtfully, or you can stumble into it through intense, messy experiences.

Three Areas of Radical Philosophy

- Communication: You need the ability to communicate so powerfully that you can influence others in extreme ways.

- Action: You need to have unwavering dedication and be willing to push forward, no matter the obstacles.

- Ideology: You need your own belief system - a solid framework of ideas that clash with the status quo to make room for something new.

It comes down to perception. For instance, "radical kindness" might not sound so bad at first. But any radical behavior, even kindness, upends the usual norms and will spark a strong reaction.

Being the First

Striving to be "the first" in any field means adopting radical traits. It demands accountability for forging a "new normal" after countless failures, lonely moments, and turmoil. Radically pushing boundaries is vital for revolutions and world progress - nothing changes without some forceful extremes.

What sets normal communication apart from radical communication? Try telling only the absolute truth to people for 30 days. Would they call you normal or extreme? Odds are, that challenge alone could transform your life experience - and that's the whole point.

- Normal: Accepted and understood by the majority.

- Radical: Uncomfortable, potentially viewed as dangerous or unrealistic - something that puts you on your own path.

The reason so many on the road to greatness feel misunderstood and have to tackle even more barriers in pursuit of goals few can comprehend is because they embrace a radical philosophy.

Shifting Between States

Any skill, value, identity, or behavior can change from normal to radical (or vice versa) - sometimes intentionally, sometimes subconsciously. Radical always implies some degree of destruction: a positive outcome might follow, but so might chaos. Before you commit to switching from normal to radical, think carefully about why. There are three layers of Impact (Figure 11):

- Personal – Most of the change occurs within you. You become a different person; people may notice but might not accept it.

- Group – Your radical choices affect large groups, such as teams, companies, or communities. (Think business leaders, coaches, or politicians.)

- Global – You transform the entire world, for better or worse, by challenging long-held systems or beliefs.

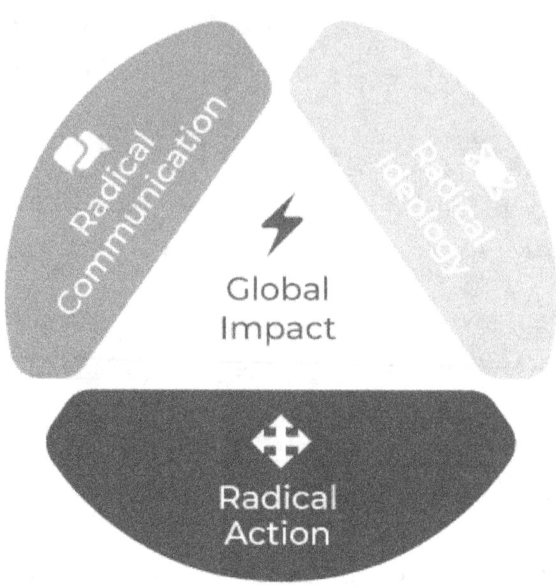

Figure 11. "Three layers of radical philosophy"

To make a group-level impact, you likely need to work on at least two of the three radical philosophy areas. A global impact requires going all in.

If you've never attempted anything radical with a positive purpose, start small - experiment with one radical trait. Try a "low-risk" version on yourself before bringing it public.

Easy Starters

Radical Communication

- Tell only the truth. (Bonus points if you carry candy for anyone who gets upset.)

- Compliment 60 strangers. Begin with their outfits, then see where conversations lead.

Radical Action

- Visit a new place each day. Especially if you live in a sprawling city.
- Cold showers. Maybe skip February unless you're in a tropical climate.

Radical Ideology

- Intermittent fasting. Bulletproof coffee can spare you from brutal hunger pangs.
- Help someone randomly. Whether with money, time, or simple attention.

The number of radical traits you adopt correlates with the scale of your Dream.

Real Examples of Radical

Personal Level – Michael Phelps: He won 28 Olympic medals - a world record. His secret? Radical discipline. The same daily routine for years might sound boring, especially to anyone with a Follower's Mindset, but it can deliver legendary results.

Group Level – Ray Dalio: One of the most successful financiers in modern history. He built a multi-billion-dollar company (Bridgewater Associates), starting from a rented apartment, and now employs thousands and advises world leaders. His secret? Radical transparency and radical principles. Meetings get recorded and shared internally; employees face a 12-month probation, after which they can't be fired.

Global Level – Elon Musk: Perhaps the most talked-about innovator today. He has turned industries experts once scoffed at, electric cars (Tesla) and rockets (SpaceX), into realities and has pushed the world closer to Mars colonization and open-sourced Tesla's patents. He's lived on a dollar a day, slept in factories, worked endless hours, and challenged high-powered figures openly. His secret? Radical Vision, dedication, and openness.

Final Thoughts

We all know effective communication is crucial. We all know massive action is needed to win. We all know great leaders form their own ideology that attracts followers. Combine all three, and you get someone with the charisma and force to shape the world.

Pick your radical traits - communication, action, or ideology - and decide how far you want to go. Tread carefully, but if your Dream is huge, a dash of radicality might be exactly what you need.

CHAPTER 17

CHALLENGES

> *"Growth is forged in discomfort. Challenges are not obstacles; they are stepping stones that test your limits, shape your resilience, and reveal the greatness within."*
> - Arnold Schwarzenegger

A challenge isn't just good - it's great.

In 2020, I took on twelve different 30-day challenges. Some changed my life, others taught me harsh lessons, and a few felt like wasted time. But collectively, it was a "blessed suffering," propelling me to a new level of Personal Maturity.

If you've never heard of a "30-Day Challenge," here's the simplest explanation:

You pick something you want to do or achieve and commit to it every single day for 30 days. If you slip and miss a day, you start over. If you make it, you might form a habit, learn a skill, or discover a new version of yourself

One challenge I did was "No Coffee for 30 Days." The outcome was so positive that I kept it going for a whole year. It taught me tons about my mental and physical health, my level of discipline, and how much energy I truly had. This was a simple challenge, yet I was surprised by the outcome - which happens almost every time I do one.

The most important lesson? Doing something daily for 30 days gives you a rough but powerful understanding of that activity or behavior. You gain enough real-life experience to ask good questions, assess causes and effects, and decide whether to continue or stop. It can save you months or even years of going in circles - overthinking something you might otherwise never try. It also reveals your physical, mental, and spiritual limits.

30-Day Challenges are fantastic Growth tools - a practical mechanism to test 12 different ideas a year, some of which could be life-altering. Maybe a certain diet, habit, or skill is right for you, but you don't want to commit long-term. This approach is like a cheat code for Transformation.

Ideally, challenges should support your Mission and Vision. Pick ones that help you make small, steady progress toward your goals. For instance, I chose 30 days without coffee because I wanted to see its impact on my health (one of my core Values). Many of my other challenges focused on health improvements, but you could diversify across physical, mental, or spiritual realms to get a broader perspective. You can also target any element of the Personal Maturity Framework, using challenges to pinpoint which ones resonate most.

Challenges are a powerful way to grow. You can tackle the Follower's Mindset, Social Debt, or Borrowed Success by shaping challenges around these problems. Combining tasks of varying difficulty and impact helps you adapt to new routines, so pick them carefully.

Recommended Starter Pack

Here's a set of challenges to create meaningful experiences that may shape your future:

- Cold Showers: Popular, high-impact, and moderately tough. You can take a cold shower every time or alternate between hot and cold. Benefits include a major energy boost, better focus, and less fatigue - you'll never feel groggy after an icy shower. It might fit with your Life Purpose or just give you a new mental edge.

- No Social Media: This can be brutal - but it comes with high rewards. It directly counters the Follower's Mindset and Social Debt from Section 1. The easiest method is to replace social media with something else (learning, self-discovery, or a daily walk). Disconnect fully and see what happens. The test of willpower alone can produce transformative insights. You may never use social media the same way again.

- No Coffee: As I mentioned, this challenge has a moderate difficulty level but a big potential impact. Expect curious (or skeptical) reactions when people find out you've quit caffeine. For me, it stabilized my sleep, lowered my blood pressure, and freed me from alarm clocks. I never anticipated all those benefits; I simply discovered a version of myself that I preferred. A challenge like this can reset your outlook on your routines.

- Meditation: This can be the simplest way to learn about yourself - with possibly the highest rewards. Think of meditation as "passive journaling." You can pair it with actual journaling for even deeper effects. It reveals how frantic your mind can be and may also expose you to higher realms of consciousness, if you let it. Each technique and experience is different, so experiment until you find one that resonates. For me, meditation unlocked a stream of new ideas - both personal and professional - and helped me come to terms with chronic pain. Let it guide you where it will.

- New Ideas: Building on the concept of a Mission, we often have cluttered thoughts. You can harness a challenge to extract the gold nuggets. For 30 days, write down 15 (or more) things you desire - every single day. Initially easy, it gets tougher as days progress. You might surprise yourself by unearthing deeply buried thoughts. It also helped me realize how many of my ideas weren't truly mine but were influenced by others. If you're feeling mentally weighed down, this challenge can help clear the noise.

This set alone could keep you busy for at least five months.

Tactics for Success

- Plan Your Environment: Make sure you have everything you need for the challenge. If you want to do a "30 days of home-cooked meals" challenge, keep travel to a minimum that month.

- Set Up Tracking: A notebook is the fastest, easiest way to log daily progress and capture your thoughts. Digital is fine, but pen and paper keeps it simple.

- Social Commitment: If you worry about giving up, tell others and ask them to check in with you. Sometimes the light pressure of accountability helps you persevere.

- Opportunity Mindset: A challenge isn't really a challenge - it's an opportunity to learn that comes with minimal cost, few time constraints, and massive potential payoff, even if it's just "300 push-ups a day."

Ultimately, you'll adopt a mindset that welcomes inevitable change and embraces it for survival. Your response to daily stress, other people, and life hardships will evolve to a new, more mature level. You'll experience mental calmness, sharper critical thinking, and improved focus on what truly matters. Each challenge is an educational experience. If you dislike the result, you can walk away with no regrets, secure in the knowledge that you tried. The investment is small; the potential relief is big.

Challenges make you feel whole - unifying your psychological harmony with a chaotic world. They return power and control to you, letting you choose how to shape your life.

Challenge is the path to change. Now, let's explore the power of Micro-Change.

CHAPTER 18

MICRO CHANGE

> *"Change is the only constant in life."*
>
> - Heraclitus

Change is coming, and it's inevitable.

The world is perpetually shifting, with or without your consent. As far as we can guess, it will keep shifting indefinitely. Our society has entire cultures - and sometimes bizarre levels of paranoia - built around the concept of change. Change is now a must in life, and this book is no exception: it's all about foundational change - finding your Life Purpose.

When handled carefully, change can be the start of a new chapter in your life. But navigating it isn't easy. You'll face three competing camps: one that idolizes radical self-development, another that adopts nihilism ("nothing matters"), and a third that Values a more balanced approach to life. It's no small task for someone who's just trying to handle a regular day job, let alone searching for Life Purpose and needing to make major changes.

In this swirl of misinformation, social conflict, and ceaseless striving for meaning, we often overthink and worry ourselves sick. Eventually, society grows anxious, depressed, and afraid - until that atmosphere becomes the new normal. Change isn't just a set of tools for moving from one state to another. First, it's a mindset. Once you learn, understand, and accept that, it becomes a playbook for Growth, meaning, and increasing Personal Maturity.

For as long as I can remember, I've belonged to the radical self-development camp, trying to push my Life boundaries in every direction. I wanted everything to continuously improve - no exceptions. I chose a mentally exhausting way of living that forced me to give up on many pursuits because I couldn't physically or emotionally keep up. Logically, I also explored other philosophies and realized none were sustainable in the long run. I'd just swing from one extreme to another, never truly understanding why I was pushing so hard for improvement. It felt like I needed to optimize everything, from washing dishes to my philosophical worldview. Great on paper, hell in practice.

That's when I started searching for patterns in different schools of thought about changing behavior, thinking, and experience. I dug into philosophy, psychology, business development, self-help, religion - pretty much everywhere. In the end, I concluded that only one approach would really work for me - a concept I call micro-change.

What Is Micro-Change?

From the name, it's the smallest change imaginable. You may have encountered similar ideas, especially in books about habits ("get 1% better every day, and in a year, you're a new person"). But micro-change isn't the same. 1% can still be a big leap for someone on an average day.

Micro-change is an organic, natural way of evolving. It's powered by consciousness and awareness. Think about all those small experiences that happen to you every day.

- Maybe a simple walk triggers playful thoughts, and suddenly you see everything differently; the person who returns from the walk isn't the same person who left.

- You might be on page 47 of some book, read a single line, and it completes a mental puzzle you didn't even know you were working on.

Micro-change is all about Life daily experiences stacking up to produce compound wisdom. It slowly forges new behaviors and yields noticeable personality Transformations. Instead of fretting about the "best technique" to lock in a habit, focus on how you really change. Start noticing each tiny moment of personal development. Recognize the sparks that shift your perception. Micro-change doesn't come from grinding or hitting 1% daily improvement goals. It emerges from understanding how change happens. Once you grasp this, you become unstoppable.

Before going deeper into why micro-change is so important or how to use it, I want you to imagine the broader structure of our world - because if you see why change has been so hard, despite everyone hyping self-improvement, life will get simpler. We often look but don't truly see. I want you to see.

The Three Elements of Existence

- You: You're the center of your personal universe. Your ego sits in the middle, influencing your decisions, actions, and perceptions of life and the people in it. At any time, you can look around at your world - and your ego is trying to run the show.

- Society: A structure built by individuals - yes, the same individuals it tries to regulate. Society strives to protect, provide, and demand. It keeps everything (more or less) running smoothly. You might dwell in your own universe, but you also need to follow society's rules (which keep evolving) to achieve your goals.

- Nature: The universal force that's expanding, changing, and pressing down on both societies and individuals. Nature sets the environment, unpredictable patterns, and conditions, constantly testing how strong we are.

You exist inside society, and society exists inside nature. All three are interconnected, an ecosystem that never stops influencing itself.

Two Types of Change

- Change We Can't Control: This includes natural disasters, cosmic events, time, death, other people's minds, social norms, and so on - things that are basically out of our hands.

- Change We Can Control: Our feelings, emotions, actions, thoughts, creativity, hunger, health, money - the list goes on. These are things we at least have some say over.

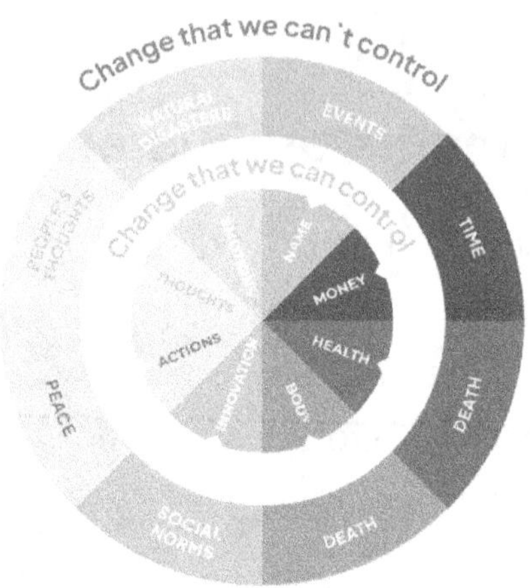

Figure 12. "Two type of changes Changes in your life"

To excel at micro-change, step one is to stop worrying. You want micro-change to be organic. Step two is releasing your sense of responsibility for the complexities of the world (the first category). Unless you're directly involved in tackling a cosmic-scale challenge - like building a rocket company - let it be. Let your curiosity watch how natural forces and massive social trends play out. Stay neutral and form your perspective as needed.

The second category is where you can make a real impact. It's connected to your ego, the center of your personal realm. Your personality craves the satisfaction of greatness - part of why you want a big Life Purpose. Micro-change, in its simplicity, activates your connection to ego, society, and nature through the smallest Transformations. It's a gentle stimulus to keep your mind curious. When you learn something new, celebrate it.

Life has so many moving pieces that it's hard to keep up. We need an easy way to handle the mental load, and micro-change is exactly that

- small, natural transitions to new states of being. Another way to grasp its simplicity: try accepting the statement, "There is no good or bad, only results." How does that feel? About 17 years ago, I realized this, and it changed my life trajectory. If life is purely about deciding which results you want or how to handle the results you already have, everything becomes clearer. No more labeling people or situations as good or bad; just target the results you desire, or adapt to the ones you didn't.

Two Short Examples

Accidentally Stepping on Someone's Foot: Is it good or bad? With a micro-change mindset, you see it's just an outcome - no need for drama. If it wasn't deliberate, there's no guilt. That's it - no moralizing needed. If you don't like the outcome (injuring someone's foot), act differently.

Getting a Year-End Bonus: Good or bad? Again, just an outcome. Sure, you'll feel happy, but that happiness might fade in a few days. That's why a bonus itself isn't inherently good or bad; it's simply the payoff for your efforts, and it might motivate you to seek bigger or more frequent payouts. If you want that to become a monthly event, you'll think about what it takes to make it happen. That's micro-change shifting your mindset away from good vs. bad thinking to focusing on outcomes and next steps.

Principles for Adopting Micro-Change

- Embrace a Life Purpose Mindset: Ideally, discover that purpose along the way (like with this book).

- Accept & Celebrate Each Micro-Change: Whether it's something small and spontaneous or a conscious tweak you initiated.

- Don't Force: Even under social or family pressure, let it happen naturally.

- Trust Your Subconscious: Let it process small wins and figure out how to move forward.

- Build Simple Routines: Give your mind time to stew on these shifts. Insights will often show up unexpectedly.

- Keep a Healthy Skepticism: Self-development isn't fake, but plenty of gurus push superficial solutions.

- Learn Inaction: Sometimes doing nothing is as powerful as taking action.

- Develop Calmness: Accept what's inevitable - like nature, time, or society's broader forces.

- Be an Observer: Remain open to micro-change moments. They often arise when you least expect.

Not everyone will vibe with micro-change. Some people need the "phoenix" moment - burning to ashes before being reborn with a new perspective. Others quietly reach a sudden insight while casually strolling down the street, ice cream in hand. You leave the house as one person and return as another, because a random thought clicked into place. That's a micro-change. Notice it. Celebrate it. Realize your personality just leveled up. Approach each Mission with an open mind, ready for these mini awakenings.

We've got a few "darker" topics ahead. Now that you've seen how to handle change positively, it's time to explore the shadow side of Growth - beginning with Solitude.

CHAPTER 19

SHADOW WORK

> *"Knowing your own darkness is the best method for dealing with the darknesses of other people."*
> — Carl Jung

What is the darkest thought that has ever crossed your mind?

Did you just really think about that!?

It happens because of the shadow - the dark side of your psyche. The shadow is your partner; your ego is its best friend.

It's time to hire your shadow for some Transformational work. True learning often comes from the deepest reaches of your mind and soul - places with no light, where monsters from our past, present, and future lurk, waiting for us to give up. Every time you consider doing something unethical or acting malevolently, your shadow appears. Driven by personal experiences or group identity, the environment around you heavily shapes how the shadow expresses itself. That's one reason Social Debt can be so dangerous. It reminds us that every human has the capacity for aggression - a survival mechanism buried by culture in favor of morality. Whenever you over-control or suppress your feelings, you feed an "inner demon" that may eventually emerge. These demons love a Follower's Mindset.

To keep them at bay, you have to learn how to express your emotions so they don't feed on your hidden frustrations, turning you into a cog in a perpetually depressed society. This "artificial persona" has two sides:

- The version of you that doesn't bother or offend anyone - so people feel free to use you for their own ends.

- The harmless facade that ultimately damages you, because one day you'll realize you wasted your life pleasing others at the expense of your own goals.

As with everything else in this book, you've got to start somewhere - ideally somewhere small. If you want an introduction to how your shadow side works, try telling the truth for 30 days, as suggested in Chapter 16. I did this and discovered very quickly that people don't actually like honest answers - despite insisting they do. Start paying attention to how you feel after each interaction. If someone appreciates your honesty, keep going; if not, then maybe share the truth only when they specifically ask for it. This one tweak releases the pent-up energy from pretending. You stop burying the negative emotions that arise from "acting nice." You may experience real emotional freedom.

In essence, Shadow Work means letting all sorts of emotions come out rather than burying them. One of my darkest periods came in 2018, after I separated from my ex-wife. Anger, sadness, regret - they all showed up at once. I'd typically numb these feelings, but this time I dared to confront them head-on, journaling my ugliest thoughts and realizing they were signposts to the parts of me I'd ignored for too long. Be sad, angry, envious, or even aggressive - situationally, of course, like in competitive sports. Learn to fully inhabit both ends of the emotional spectrum. Crying and laughing both matter for a healthy mind. Don't let others discourage you from expressing what you feel - body language, facial expressions, all of it. Let it flow out of you. And be ready to listen too, so you can talk things through instead of letting them fester.

Why the Shadow Matters

The shadow's concept is pivotal for Life Purpose and Personal Maturity. Ignoring it slices your potential in half. Society often encourages only the "positive" emotions, painting negative ones as unacceptable. But acting invulnerable is pointless. We can't pretend there's no evil in us. Sometimes, in extreme uncertainty or danger, so-called negative emotions - anger, rage - might literally save your life or someone else's. Nature may push you past your comfort zone to spark primal instincts. You should know your own capacity, which Shadow Work reveals.

Observing, exploring, integrating, and applying shadow principles improves your Life Design. Yes, it's difficult. There's no neat recipe for dealing with the inner void because its depth varies from person to person. Still, here are recognized steps to begin (Figure 13):

- Awareness: Watch your behaviors, emotions, and thoughts. Get curious about yourself. Jot down mental notes.

- Discovery: Challenge your Vision, Mission, Values, and Qualities. Hold an inner dialogue to uncover root causes. Keep asking "why" and "what for" until things start to click.

- Integration: Channel your "negative" energy into something positive - sports, art, public speaking - anything that lets you productively harness your darker urges. Practice without harming others (or yourself).

- Acceptance: Recognize you have a shadow, that it shows itself in different ways, and that you're still learning to manage it. Share this acknowledgment with those close to you so they can respond more constructively. It can really minimize conflict and judgment.

Figure 13. "Steps for Shadow Work"

Carl Jung, the Swiss psychiatrist and psychoanalyst who founded analytical psychology, introduced the formal idea of the shadow. After his break with Freud in 1913, he went through a major crisis - personally and professionally. He delved into his unconscious, which evolved into The Red Book. Even Jung started by acknowledging his shadow, seeing that everyone denies certain parts of themselves because society labels them unacceptable. He'd suppressed a host of fears, desires, and other ignored aspects of his life, then discovered he could become whole by channeling that "dark" energy into conscious endeavors instead of burying it. He accepted his shadow as a genuine part of his psyche.

When you truly learn Shadow Work, you might even talk with your shadow through Dream. Your Dream will nudge you about what's really important and can guide you.

The Power of "No"

Another huge piece of Shadow Work is dealing with rejection - and learning how to reject others' ideas, requests, negativity, and anything that doesn't feed your Life Purpose. The simplest way is to say "No" more often. This can be psychologically intense. Telling someone no means you refuse to do what they want. In that moment, you're essentially saying they can't force you - and your capacity for aggression (the shadow) is an unspoken backdrop to that stance. People often struggle to say no because they fear another's aggressive response or because their own shadow isn't robust enough. But "No" is key for developing a healthy shadow. Telling the truth, saying no, letting emotions flow, and practicing Shadow Work aren't easy, but you can grow faster by testing your extremes. You need to see the full range of your potential. Some of it might be easier in solitude, which we'll discuss soon.

Tips for Engaging Your Shadow

- Don't Bottle Up Your Feelings: Learn what you truly want - even if it's unethical or impossible. If you're constantly denied what you want, you risk developing destructive coping habits. So figure out your real desires and find a safe way to address them.

- Stop Judging Others: If you're tempted to mock someone's insecurities, remember you're often projecting your own.

Each time you want to blame them, pause and consult your "shadow mirror." Is it actually your unfulfilled potential or a hidden monster talking?

- Never Abuse Your Power: It can feel satisfying in the moment, but it clouds your judgment. That's not genuine Shadow Work; it's fake dominance. Instead, think about why you crave that power boost and what you're masking.

- Don't Play the Victim: Accept accountability for your existence.

Be open to both the light and the dark aspects of yourself, without crossing a line that hurts others. You'll sense greater freedom and create more capacity for achievement.

The "Wall of Truth" Tactic

Here's another method to unearth your deeper secrets - about yourself and others. By now, you should have a clearer idea of your Vision and Mission. To create your Wall of Truth, write down your immediate goal:

- Ask Why: Why do you want this? Record your reasons.

- Ask Why Again: Direct this question at your reason itself. Why do you need that reason?

- Repeat: Go several layers deep until you can't move forward without relying on vague philosophy or until you run out of patience.

- You'll usually find multiple layers of "why":

- The first layer is the socially acceptable reason.

- The second layer is a bit less acceptable but still shareable with close friends.

- The third might be a secret known only to a tiny circle.

- The fourth is known only to yourself.

- The fifth is something you're too ashamed to admit, even to yourself.

Beyond that is pure darkness, where few dare to tread. The Wall of Truth helps expose your shadow in those deeper layers, revealing what you truly desire. Without confronting it, your Life Design and Life Purpose might stay incomplete or less potent.

Become Whole Again

You were born to create a unique story, but Life challenges, society, and the world pushed away and diminished bits of your personality. You learned to be "acceptable" by burying uncomfortable emotions and losing sight of your purpose. The shadow is part of the game, and all emotions need space. Otherwise, we pretend there's no darkness and mistake harmlessness for virtue - becoming inauthentic so others will like us instead of really understanding us. That yields an obedient society afraid of critical thinking, terrified of judgment, and always hiding from self-truth.

Shadow Work lets you recover those missing parts, showing you who you really are and why your hunger for greatness is valid. A fully integrated personality can handle Life challenges - and reach the Big Dream.

Explore your dark side. Partner with your shadow to finally become you.

CHAPTER 20

SOLITUDE

> *"Solitude gives birth to the original in us, to beauty unfamiliar and perilous - to poetry."*
>
> — Thomas Mann

Solitude is powerful - if you can afford it financially, spiritually, mentally and psychologically.

In 2019, I was fortunate enough to isolate myself for thirty days. I'd just moved from Long Island to New York City after separating from my ex-wife, and I had the opportunity to stay home for a while. I needed space to think, so I dove headfirst into Self-Discovery and Self-Reflection.

I was at a tough point in my life, and this experiment felt right - mentally and physically. Sometimes you just know. I had zero hesitation. I wanted to explore my inner world, darkness included.

I sensed that hidden stuff was lurking in my psyche, waiting for me to confront it. So I created the space for intense introspection, and it turned out to be the perfect environment for Shadow Work, which we'll explore soon. For now, I'll skip the logistics and share what I learned.

Working on the shadow side of your personality is just as vital as developing your Vision, Mission, Values, Qualities, and Growth Identity. A life without it is incomplete. Tons of psychological evidence supports the value of self-reflection, especially concerning your "dark" side - and solitude offers the ideal backdrop. After trying it myself, I recommend solitude in smaller doses, like a few days or even just 24 hours. It can work wonders, giving you a chance to truly meet yourself. In our noisy world, finding even a single "empty day" feels nearly impossible. Our bustling cities are filled with lonely people who stay busy simply to avoid feeling alone.

Your initial impression of isolation might resemble a sandstorm sweeping through a deserted city: without the usual distractions, your mind wanders into unexpected territory. Old memories, random emotions, and Vision of potential futures all bubble up. Your brain, starved of attention, throws everything it's got at you. This is your chance to talk with yourself. Tools like journaling or meditation can help you gather and organize your avalanche of thoughts. I did video journaling, basically talking to myself at the end of each day. I pulled out a lot of deep stuff - some of it very personal, and I'll share a bit here.

Solitude & The Dark Side

First and foremost, you should aim for brutally honest self-reflection. You might dislike, be disappointed by, or even try to hide from what you discover - don't. No one's watching. This is the perfect moment to accept who you are. To show you the depth of this work, here's some of what I learned about myself:

- Over the years, I'd become quite narcissistic. I craved attention from everyone while giving almost nothing back.

- Even with a strong career, I still feared authority. I was fine being lazy in my personal life but felt intense guilt if I slacked at work - especially around senior figures. Consequently, I never knew how to say "no."

- Sometimes I had fake confidence. If anyone challenged my competence - even kindly - I'd become defensive and push them away.

- I pursued perfection to a fault. Anything short of perfection really bothered me, making me an intense leader to work with.

- My emotional stability was questionable; my mood swings could catch even my closest friends off guard.

- I struggled to learn from others. I'd pick mentors I personally liked, without verifying their expertise, leading to needless blunders.

- Because I couldn't say "no," I'd juggle a double agenda: outwardly agreeable, inwardly rebellious, as I childishly coped with stress.

- Even though I was decisive, I would often contradict myself - my belief system might shift multiple times a week. My tolerance for others' perspectives was minimal.

Reading this, you might challenge the notion that I'm "good" or "successful." It sounds monstrous - selfish, ignorant, greedy. If people dealt with that every day, no wonder I sometimes got negative outcomes.

What if I'd never done this solitude experiment? The revelations were overwhelming and hard to accept, and even now, I'm still fixing some of it. Your story might be different, but be prepared. Without tackling your major blind spots, it's much harder to handle the Follower's Mindset, Social Debt, Borrowed Success, or any Life Purpose Transformation. How deeply you dig depends on how free you let your mind roam.

I learned that solitude is part of Personal Maturity.

Solitude & Potential

Despite uncovering a rough "dark side," solitude also shines light on your bright side. You do have potential for greatness, and your mind will remind you of past promises and half-forgotten Dream that still fit into your purpose-driven life. You'll recall who you wanted to be and find new sparks for the future. This is the flip side of all the dark revelations - bright ideas waiting to be claimed.

By now, I hope you have a decent grasp of your Life Design elements. That structure will help you filter your mind's noise and enforce discipline as you decide what to act on. Some bright ideas might need a fully developed Growth Mindset, while others will just require a spark to remind you of your inherent power. Here are a few tips:

- There's no instruction manual for being alone. Expect tough emotional moments and see them through.

- Everyone must go through this process alone. It genuinely fortifies you.

- Personal Maturity happens when you battle scary mental monsters - one at a time.

- You can't discover meaning in life if you're always busy. Chores and tasks can wait while you soul-search.

- No one has all the answers to every "why."

- We have a creator's mind - capable of building entire worlds, literally or figuratively.

- Feeling sad is okay; it's a catalyst for change, nudging you toward the bright side.

- Regret often arrives too late. Don't waste potentially great moments because of pointless social media scrolling or endless work meetings.

- Ditch your backup plans. You might lose yourself by trying to satisfy everything and everyone.

Solitude & Productivity

Using what you learned about Micro-Changes and Challenges, solitude becomes easier to understand. It fosters courage, invites risk, and transforms chaos into order. It's the ultimate productivity hack. If you remove external noise, you finally have the time for what matters.

For me, that includes traveling, reading, dayDreaming, building confidence, and trying new stuff. Solitude has helped me swap "working hard" (often doing what other people wanted) for focused work (centered on what I want - still within social norms). Solitude clarifies your priorities so you can drop unimportant tasks. If you recall Chapter 7's Mission exercise, you can use that approach to see what to keep or discard. Here are some of my productivity discoveries, which you can apply even without total solitude:

- Keep a system - one central place to track your tasks.

- Stop giving "advice" unless asked. (Some exceptions apply, of course.)

- Make time for in-depth thinking about tough issues - and invite others in when needed.

- Don't force yourself or others to change. Self-development is inherently slow; don't let any self-help books rush your process.

- Aim for financial freedom as a key Mission so you can afford to explore your purpose.

- Use challenges consistently because daily life can be too safe and distract you from important self-questions.

- Advance by focusing on one important thing a day. Watch out for mental exhaustion from task-switching.

- It's easier to give others advice than to confront your own areas of Growth - learn to listen to you.

Solitude & the Unknown

Each solitude experiment yields observations you can't immediately interpret. Stay calm. Jot them down. Answers come through direct efforts or through micro-changes that unfold as you tackle your Mission. It could be the first time you've had a one-on-one with yourself. Don't quit if you don't morph into some sagely guru on day one or, if halfway through, you feel overwhelmed. Stay humble, keep an open mind, and maybe try again later.

Some questions still puzzle me, even after years doing this work:

- How do you celebrate a huge win If no one's around to share it with?

- Could you achieve emotional balance by slowing down decisions, feelings, and desires?

- You'll have experiences no one else will ever know. Can you still enjoy life while you keep secrets locked away?

Solitude & Readiness

Finally, solitude teaches you how to handle what you previously couldn't. Maybe the answer was always right there; you just never had the time or courage to see it. You might feel overwhelmed at first, so keep that journal close.

Accept that you might not know yourself well. Facing your shadow can be uncomfortable. Silence is hard but necessary. You won't conquer all your fears in one go, but you can note them down and tackle them later. As I said at the start, solitude is powerful if you can afford it. Such freedom can be risky - who knows, maybe you'll emerge wanting to revamp your entire life. That's why I recommend starting with short stints of solitude unless you're ready for a massive upheaval.

The quality of your solitude depends on your relationship with yourself - your inner voice will judge you every minute. Typically, we numb that voice with our phones, social events, or anything that blocks out self-awareness. Eventually, you can't ignore it if you want to make real progress. This was easier for me because I grew up pretty introverted. No big prep was needed - I sensed I could manage my alone time. Interestingly, solitude also unlocked an extroverted side of me, making me open to new experiences. It's a thorough test of readiness on multiple levels and can deeply enrich your Life Design and Personal Maturity. After all, we function in patterns, and the world offers a thousand ways to stretch us in different directions.

To discover your Life Purpose, you have to control aspects of yourself that you might never have considered. The outside world will keep pulling you everywhere, so your Mission is to find the potential you can fulfill - and then dive into the darkest corners of your mind to retrieve the answers.

Time to wrap things up.

AFTERTHOUGHTS

> *"When I let go of what I am, I become what I might be."*
>
> — Lao Tzu

You made it. Welcome to the other side - congratulations.

This journey has probably been challenging and anything but linear, but like every adventure, it's simply a prelude to an even bigger one that's waiting just around the corner. Now is the time for you to regroup and continue taking practical steps toward the Life Purpose you've crafted.

You've learned that the Follower's Mindset, Social Debt, and Borrowed Success pose some of the biggest obstacles for many people. You've also learned that Life Design - with its Vision, Mission, Values, Qualities, and Growth Identity - is a powerful way to break free from these obstacles by channeling your focus on a Big Dream. Beyond that, you've discovered Personal Maturity, a holistic framework for a meaningful life built on four categories: Life Design, Social Success, Personal Efficiency, and Transformation. This framework equips you to handle the world's complexity and take accountability for your own existence.

You've also explored strategies and tactics from the Personal Maturity Framework to apply to your unique situation. Among others:

- Dream Big - It's essential.

- Design and Control Your Purpose - Own your Vision and Mission.

- Measure and Understand Your Maturity - Do it regularly.

- Plan for New Challenges at Every Maturity Level - Build systems to tackle them.

- Embrace Negative Emotions - They're the parts of your life you've pushed away. Integrate them to become whole.

Ultimately, this book encourages you to Dream Big, form a Life Design to chase your Life Purpose, and then bolster your Personal Maturity to overcome any challenges.

This is my attempt to give you a logical structure with practical steps for building and sustaining a meaningful life. I always knew I'd write a book at some point - I just wasn't sure what form it would take. Now that it's done, it feels like I've consolidated all my knowledge, wisdom, and ideas, giving closure to one phase of my life so I can transition to the next. This, too, is a Personal Maturity Journey for me, and finishing this book feels like making a personal statement   I can turn the page, something I've badly needed. I've extracted everything I know and put it down in words. I've exposed myself, showing who I truly am and what I believe. This is me. This book is me. I've written down everything I know so I can move forward unencumbered.

I never mentioned this directly, but my Life Purpose is to Achieve Absolute Freedom. I want to be free from the financial burdens of the rat race - which includes genuinely valuing what I already have and never chasing money again. I want to be free from social judgment, letting go of recognition, approval, and the pressure to conform to any system. I want to breathe freely and make decisions unaffected by outside forces. I want to accomplish great, meaningful things without being tangled up in the pursuit of glory. I want to explore new great things and find what no one else has. I want to share whatever wisdom I gather so others can also do amazing things and we can all see how far humanity can go. I want to keep a childlike curiosity about life - and not fear wandering off my path. Ultimately, I want to break free even from life itself, aiming to be absolutely free.

Thank you for joining me on this journey.

APPENDIX A. PERSONAL MATURITY FRAMEWORK

This framework is divided into four major categories - Life Design, Social Success, Personal Efficiency, and Transformation - with 24 total elements. Each element has 6 maturity levels (0 to 5). Level 0 represents minimal awareness or development, while Level 5 suggests mastery, global impact, or a fully integrated practice. Use these descriptions to identify your current level in each element and see what steps might help you move forward.

How to Use This Framework

- Self-Assessment: For each element, read the level descriptions (0–5) and identify the one that resonates most with your current situation.

- Goal-Setting: Note the gap between your current level and a desired level. What specific actions or habits could bridge that gap?

- Continuous Review: Revisit your self-assessment periodically - every 6 or 12 months - to track changes and adjust your focus.

- Integration: Combine multiple elements. For instance, if your Wealth is at Level 1 but your Financial System is at Level 2, you can plan synergy between them.

- Celebrate Progress: Acknowledge each step upward. Even moving from Level 1 to Level 2 can mark a significant shift in mindset.

This Appendix is meant to be a practical guide. Adapt these descriptions to your personal context, and remember that Growth in one element can often catalyze improvements in others. Each small step, consistently taken, will move you forward on your Personal Maturity Journey.

LIFE DESIGN	
Element: Vision	
Description:	Your Vision is your guiding star - the compelling picture of what you want your future to look like. A strong Vision propels you forward and inspires both you and those around you.
Level 0:	No real Vision. May feel directionless and have little motivation for the future.
Level 1:	Beginning to sense a need for direction. Exploring possibilities and Dreaming about what the future could hold.
Level 2:	Beginning to sense a need for direction. Exploring possibilities and Dreaming about what the future could hold. Have some clarity on what you want, but it's still vague. Seeking ways to refine and articulate that Vision more concretely
Level 3:	A well-defined Vision you feel excited about. Actively shaping goals and plans around i well-defined Vision you feel excited about. Actively shaping goals and plans around it.
Level 4:	Fully committed to and recognized for your clarity of purpose. People may look to you for inspiration
Level 5:	Visionary leader who influences others on a larger scale - helping others create and pursue their own Visions.
Element: Mission	
Description:	Your Mission is the specific idea behind your Big Dream, capturing your potential impact on the world. A clear Mission aligns your actions with your Values, providing a sense of meaning

Level 0:	No sense of purpose. Feeling lost and unmotivated.
Level 1:	In the self-discovery stage - curious about potential contributions but unsure where to start.
Level 2:	Have a general sense of Mission, and explore different paths that fit your Dream and Values.
Level 3:	Clear Mission and full commitment. Developing skills and knowledge to fulfill it.
Level 4:	Mission largely realized, with significant accomplishments. Possibly mentoring or guiding others on similar paths.
Level 5:	Beyond personal Mission - creating a broad positive impact and inspiring collective change.

Element: Values

Description:	Your Values are the core principles and beliefs that guide your decisions, define your character, and reflect what truly matters to you. They shape how you navigate moral dilemmas and interpersonal relationships.
Level 0:	Unaware or disconnected from personal Values. Often confused about right vs. wrong in daily life.
Level 1:	Beginning to question what truly matters. Exploring various philosophies or moral systems.
Level 2:	Gaining clarity on essential Values and trying to incorporate them into everyday decisions.
Level 3:	Strongly grounded in a set of personal Values. Consistently aligns choices with those Values.
Level 4:	Values deeply integrated. May serve as an example for others, demonstrating integrity in challenging situations.
Level 5:	Living your Values seamlessly, regardless of external pressures. Actively promotes value-based living in communities or organizations.

Element: Qualities

Description:	Qualities refer to the inherent traits - like discipline, accountability, passion, consistency, and open-mindedness - that shape how you operate in the world. Developing these Qualities fosters success and resilience.
Level 0:	Lacks self-awareness of personal strengths or traits. Tends toward negative behaviors.
Level 1:	Beginning to reflect on personal Qualities. Seeking feedback or self-help resources.
Level 2:	Recognizes specific strengths and weaknesses. Actively works on improving limiting Qualities.
Level 3:	Demonstrates consistent, positive traits (e.g., discipline, responsibility). Gains respect from peers for character.
Level 4:	Displays a high level of self-mastery in most Qualities. Often sought out as a role model or mentor.

Level 5:	Exemplary character recognized beyond immediate circles. Uses well-honed Qualities to uplift communities or teams globally.

Element: Growth Identity

Description:	Identity is your sense of self - the combination of experiences, beliefs, roles, and personal narratives that define "who you are." A stable yet flexible identity supports Growth, authenticity, and confidence.
Level 0:	Little sense of personal identity. May feel lost, imitating others to fit in.
Level 1:	Beginning to question who you are. Might try different "versions" of self.
Level 2:	Gaining clarity on personal roles and beliefs. Feeling more settled in how you present yourself.
Level 3:	Strong identity. Comfortable with who you are while remaining open to evolve further.
Level 4:	Identity is deeply rooted and resilient. Others see you as "grounded" or "authentic."
Level 5:	A self-actualized identity that transcends roles. You help others discover their own sense of self confidently.

SOCIAL SUCCESS
Element: Health

Description:	Health is the foundation of well-being - physical, emotional, and mental. By focusing on nutrition, exercise, rest, and stress management, you enhance your vitality and longevity
Level 0:	Little or no attention to physical, mental, or emotional health. Unhealthy habits dominate.
Level 1:	Aware of the need to improve health, but struggling to begin. Might feel overwhelmed.
Level 2:	Making some steps (exercise, diet changes) but lacking consistency. Improvement is sporadic.
Level 3:	Actively prioritizing health. Developing balanced habits and making noticeable progress.
Level 4:	Master of body and mind. Your healthy lifestyle is consistent, possibly inspiring those around you.
Level 5:	Champion of healthy living. Advocating for health-related causes or supporting communities in well-being initiatives.

Element: Wealth

Description:	Wealth goes beyond money to encompass abundance in all aspects of life - freedom, flexibility, security, and generosity. Building wealth involves disciplined money management, investing, and a mindset of abundance.

Level 0:	Financial instability or high debt. Limited money management skills.
Level 1:	Recognizes financial well-being's importance but unsure where to start.
Level 2:	Taking initial steps - budgeting, small savings, learning basic investing. Inconsistent but trying.
Level 3:	Committed to saving, investing, reducing debt. Achieving a stable financial platform.
Level 4:	Attained significant financial success or expertise. Continuing to build wealth or legacy.
Level 5:	Financial independence. Engaged in philanthropy or major investments. Money no longer drives decisions.

Element: Family

Description:	Family provides love, support, and moral grounding. Strong family relationships can boost resilience and give a sense of belonging. Cultivating empathy, communication, and healthy boundaries is key.
Level 0:	Neglects family relationships or responsibilities. Feels distant or disconnected.
Level 1:	Desires stronger family bonds but hasn't acted yet. Possibly reconnecting with relatives.
Level 2:	Actively building positive relationships. Spending time and prioritizing family needs.
Level 3:	Family is a top priority. Overcomes conflicts, invests in support and quality interaction.
Level 4:	Maintains deeply rooted, healthy family ties. Serves as a role model for supportive relationships.
Level 5:	Impact extends beyond your own family - contributing to community or social initiatives that benefit families broadly.

Element: Friends

Description:	Friendships enrich your emotional well-being and foster mutual Growth. Friends celebrate successes and offer stability during hardships. Building and maintaining strong friendships require openness and mutual support.
Level 0:	No active friendships; feels isolated or disconnected.
Level 1:	Attempting to find or rebuild a social circle but with limited progress.
Level 2:	Has a few solid friends. Working on building more meaningful connections.
Level 3:	Friendship is a significant part of your life - actively nurturing close relationships.
Level 4:	Long-standing, positive friendships. Consistent support and shared life experiences.
Level 5:	Deeply fulfilling friendships that benefit not only you but also help others learn how to cultivate strong bonds.

<table>
<tr><td colspan="2" align="center">Element: Relationship</td></tr>
<tr><td>Description:</td><td>Romantic or intimate relationships bring companionship, love, and Growth. Developing trust, empathy, and healthy communication fosters stability and deeper bonding.</td></tr>
<tr><td>Level 0:</td><td>No focus on forming relationships. Possibly struggles with or avoids closeness.</td></tr>
<tr><td>Level 1:</td><td>Seeking a relationship or clarity on personal needs, but lacking success or alignment.</td></tr>
<tr><td>Level 2:</td><td>Currently in a relationship but feeling it could improve. Aware of the need for better communication.</td></tr>
<tr><td>Level 3:</td><td>Committed to nurturing a healthy relationship. Resolving conflicts and building trust.</td></tr>
<tr><td>Level 4:</td><td>Strong, positive partnership with open dialogue and shared goals. Continuously improving together.</td></tr>
<tr><td>Level 5:</td><td>Mastered relationship dynamics - deep intimacy and understanding. Often helps others with relationship advice.</td></tr>
<tr><td colspan="2" align="center">Element: Hobby</td></tr>
<tr><td>Description:</td><td>A Hobby brings enjoyment and purpose beyond work or obligations. It can reduce stress, spark creativity, and boost overall happiness. Cultivating a hobby regularly is important for mental balance.</td></tr>
<tr><td>Level 0:</td><td>No real hobbies or interests. Life may feel dull or aimless outside of obligations.</td></tr>
<tr><td>Level 1:</td><td>Experimenting with various hobbies but no clear direction or consistent practice.</td></tr>
<tr><td>Level 2:</td><td>Find one or two hobbies you enjoy, starting to invest time and resources.</td></tr>
<tr><td>Level 3:</td><td>Making steady progress, improving skills in chosen hobbies, setting personal goals.</td></tr>
<tr><td>Level 4:</td><td>High level of mastery or recognition in a hobby. Possibly seen as an 'expert' or community leader.</td></tr>
<tr><td>Level 5:</td><td>Innovating or contributing significantly in hobby spaces. Possibly organizing events or training others.</td></tr>
<tr><td colspan="2" align="center">Element: Job & Career</td></tr>
<tr><td>Description:</td><td>Work provides financial stability, intellectual stimulation, and a sense of purpose. Aligning your career path with personal Values and interests fosters fulfillment.</td></tr>
<tr><td>Level 0:</td><td>Lacks direction or passion in professional life. Unfulfilled or stagnant.</td></tr>
<tr><td>Level 1:</td><td>Exploring career options or trying different roles.</td></tr>
<tr><td>Level 2:</td><td>Committed to learning and skill-building. Prioritizes professional Growth.</td></tr>
<tr><td>Level 3:</td><td>Clear on career goals, seizing opportunities for advancement or mastery.</td></tr>
<tr><td>Level 4:</td><td>High success and satisfaction. Recognized expertise or leadership in your field.</td></tr>
</table>

Level 5:	Global recognition. Committed to elevating others' careers and shaping the industry's future.

PERSONAL EFFICIENCY

Element: Learning System

Description:	Continuous learning is the engine of personal development - keeping your mind sharp and open. Focusing on acquiring new skills, knowledge, and experiences fuels long-term Growth.
Level 0:	No drive for learning. Shows little curiosity or motivation.
Level 1:	Exploring various subjects or methods but inconsistently. Lacks discipline or routine.
Level 2:	Actively prioritizing new skills or knowledge. Setting some learning goals.
Level 3:	Incorporates learning into daily life. Challenges are seen as Growth opportunities.
Level 4:	Recognized expertise in chosen domains. Regularly invests In advanced education.
Level 5:	Shares knowledge widely - mentoring, teaching, or supporting initiatives that help others learn.

Element: Planning System

Description:	A robust planning system helps structure your goals, tasks, and time. Clarity in planning minimizes wasted effort and keeps you moving forward.
Level 0:	No real planning or goal-setting. Drifts without direction.
Level 1:	Experimenting with different planning approaches but lacks consistency or follow-through.
Level 2:	Actively working on setting goals and timelines. Sees the value of a planning routine.
Level 3:	Planning is woven into daily life. You have predictable methods to manage tasks and priorities.
Level 4:	Highly organized. Rarely misses deadlines. People may admire your organizational skills.
Level 5:	The planning system is a strategic pillar. It propels large-scale projects, reduces stress, and you teach others efficient planning.

Element: Execution System

Description:	Execution turns plans into reality. It's about taking action, maintaining discipline, and persistently finishing what you start.
Level 0:	Procrastination or lack of follow-through. Goals stay on paper
Level 1:	Trying various productivity hacks or motivation tips but inconsistent.

Level 2:	Actively working on forming habits to get things done. Seeking steady improvement.
Level 3:	Execution is part of your routine. You handle challenges with determination.
Level 4:	High productivity and efficiency. Achieves goals reliably.
Level 5:	Radical action is second nature. Almost nothing derails you, and you guide others on how to execute effectively.

Element: Financial System

Description:	A personal financial system stabilizes your money situation, supports big goals, and offers freedom. It includes budgeting, saving, investing, and understanding risk.
Level 0:	Deep debt or severe financial instability. Minimal money skills.
Level 1:	Acknowledges the need for financial control; reading resources but struggling to apply.
Level 2:	Building a financial plan, starting to grow capital or reduce debt.
Level 3:	Financially stable, optimizing strategies. Possibly investing or saving for long-term wealth.
Level 4:	High financial knowledge and success. People may consult you on finance.
Level 5:	Financial freedom. Using wealth to help others or fund large-scale ventures.

Element: Productivity System

Description:	Productivity systems help you manage your time, energy, and focus. They let you accomplish more while maintaining balance, reducing stress, and keeping you aligned with larger goals.
Level 0:	Disorganized, no priority management, and often overwhelmed.
Level 1:	Trying random productivity methods but not consistently following any. Easily demotivated.
Level 2:	Committing to structured productivity habits, seeing some gains.
Level 3:	Productivity is integrated into daily life. You handle tasks efficiently and adapt to obstacles.
Level 4:	Highly effective. Consistent track record of achieving goals and staying motivated with minimal friction.
Level 5:	A "well-oiled engine" of productivity. All your systems align toward a north star, and you help others build similar frameworks.

TRANSFORMATION
Element: Ideology

Description:	Ideology is the set of beliefs and principles guiding your actions. A clear ideology fosters integrity and keeps you grounded, even under social or cultural pressure.
Level 0:	Little awareness of personal beliefs or Values. May feel aimless or easily swayed.
Level 1:	Starting to question or explore various viewpoints. Curious but not yet committed.
Level 2:	Developing a cohesive set of Values/beliefs. Testing them in real-life situations.
Level 3:	Strong ideological grounding. You align decisions with these core beliefs consistently.
Level 4:	Recognized as someone who stands firmly by your principles. Potential influence in a community.
Level 5:	Your ideology shapes broader discourse. You may lead or inspire movements aligned with your beliefs.

Element: Chaos

Description:	Chaos represents your capacity to handle the unpredictable and maintain internal order amidst external upheaval. Embracing chaos can lead to innovation and adaptability rather than stress and panic.
Level 0:	Overwhelmed by disruptions or sudden changes. Paralyzed by unpredictability.
Level 1:	Acknowledges that chaos exists but struggles to cope. May seek structure or external help.
Level 2:	Building initial resilience strategies - like simple routines or stress management - for chaotic situations
Level 3:	Manages chaos calmly. You adapt swiftly and keep a level head during major shifts.
Level 4:	Thrives in chaotic environments, using them as opportunities for creativity or progress.
Level 5:	Uses chaos as a catalyst for personal and group Transformation. Mentors others to find order in disorder.

Element: Shadow

Description:	Shadow refers to the unacknowledged or suppressed parts of your psyche - fears, desires, negative emotions - that society (or you) deems unacceptable. Integrating the shadow leads to wholeness and authentic self-expression.
Level 0:	Completely denies or represses negative feelings. May explode under pressure.
Level 1:	Notices dark impulses or emotions but avoids confronting them.
Level 2:	Attempts self-reflection or therapy. Gains partial awareness of hidden traits.

Level 3:	Actively works on shadow integration - journaling, honest conversations, controlled emotional expression.
Level 4:	Embraces the shadow as part of self, productively channeling "negative" emotions. Viewed by others as deeply self-aware.
Level 5:	Master of Shadow Work. You teach or guide others in reconciling their own dark sides, fostering collective Growth.

Element: Personality

Description:	Personality is a blend of traits, behaviors, and patterns that define how you think, act, and relate to the world. Strengthening personality involves self-awareness, emotional intelligence, and consistent reflection.
Level 0:	Little awareness of personal traits. Possibly harmful or destructive behaviors.
Level 1:	Starting to explore personality traits. Accepting feedback from others.
Level 2:	Recognizing the impact of your traits on your relationships and life choices. Trying to grow.
Level 3:	Actively improving limiting traits. Seeking resources or support for positive change.
Level 4:	High emotional intelligence and self-awareness. Manages emotions effectively.
Level 5:	Uses a developed personality to benefit society. Possibly an advocate of emotional intelligence or self-awareness initiatives.

Element: Micro Change

Description:	Micro-Change is the art of transforming yourself through small, consistent shifts in behavior or perspective. It Values cumulative wisdom and progress over drastic, short-lived overhauls.
Level 0:	Resists any form of change - prefers comfort and routine, even if unproductive.
Level 1:	Acknowledges the need for gradual change but lacks strategy or consistency.
Level 2:	Taking small steps, trying out tiny habits or daily improvements. Sees modest results.
Level 3:	Embraces micro-changes as a normal approach. Turns challenges into learning opportunities.
Level 4:	Regularly uses micro-changes to tackle big goals. Experiencing significant personal Growth
Level 5:	Expert at harnessing micro-changes. Teaches or advocates this methodology publicly, showing others how small steps lead to big Transformations.

Element: Influence

Description:	Influence is your capacity to inspire and move others toward a particular idea, goal, or action. Strong influence combines clear communication, empathy, and genuine leadership.

Level 0:	Struggles to communicate or persuade. Little awareness of how to impact others.
Level 1:	Reading or learning about influence techniques. Slowly testing them in small ways.
Level 2:	Building trust in personal/professional settings. Improving relationships via better communication.
Level 3:	Developing versatile influence skills. People often look to you for guidance or direction.
Level 4:	Skilled at motivating and inspiring others in complex situations. Recognized for effective persuasion.
Level 5:	Influence is used for broad, positive change. May spearhead initiatives or movements that benefit society.

Element: Challenges

Description:	Challenges are invitations to grow, test limits, and learn resilience. By setting ambitious goals or tackling discomfort, you sharpen your skills and gain confidence.
Level 0:	Avoids challenges entirely. Feels overwhelmed or anxious at the idea of struggle.
Level 1:	Accepts that challenges are necessary but not sure how to face them.
Level 2:	Taking small steps to confront obstacles in personal or professional life
Level 3:	Persistently navigates setbacks and bounces back quickly. Develops strong resilience.
Level 4:	Sees challenges as opportunities to innovate or grow. Often overcomes barriers efficiently.
Level 5:	Embraces 30-day challenges - or similarly rigorous tests - as a way of life. Helps others adopt challenge-based Growth.

The Personal Maturity Framework is not meant to be a rigid set of rules. Life is dynamic, and growth rarely happens in a straight line. You may find yourself strong in one element while struggling in another, or advancing in some areas while circling back in others. That's normal - maturity is a journey.

Use this framework as a mirror: to see yourself more clearly, to notice patterns, and to guide intentional change. Return to it whenever you feel lost, stuck, or ready for the next stage of growth. Over time, it can become both a roadmap and a record of how far you've come.

ABOUT THE AUTHOR

Artem Gonchakov is an entrepreneur, business leader, writer, and lifelong explorer of what it means to live with purpose. His path has been anything but straight: he has crossed countries, built companies from scratch, led global teams, and closed multimillion-dollar deals. Yet, behind the milestones, he often wrestled with the same questions many people carry quietly: What am I really doing this for? Whose definition of success am I chasing?

That search - sometimes inspiring, sometimes messy - became the heartbeat of this book. Artem wrote Unrefined - Find Your Purpose not as a polished "expert," but as someone who has stumbled, recalibrated, and grown through trial and error. His story moves through the uncertainty of immigration, the weight of social expectations, the grind of corporate life, and the chaos of entrepreneurship. He knows what it feels like to follow paths set by others, and what it takes to step off them to carve your own.

Outside the pages of this book, Artem leads Simplifai, an AI company transforming how insurers handle complex claims, and founded Arty Finch, a platform that helps startups measure maturity and grow with clarity. But business is only part of the picture. He has also tested himself in marathons, reflected in solitude after major life changes, and built frameworks that blend philosophy with lived experience.

For Artem, purpose is not a secret waiting to be found - it is something created through choices, habits, and courage. His writing reflects that: candid, unpolished, and deeply human. With Unrefined, he invites readers to question the borrowed scripts they've been handed, to face the chaos within and around them, and to begin creating a life that is truly theirs.

Connect with Artem

Website: https://www.artyfinch.com/

LinkedIn: https://www.linkedin.com/in/artem-gonchakov/

REFERENCES

Books & Memoirs

- Brown, Brené. Daring Greatly: How the Courage to Be Vulnerable Transforms the Way We Live, Love, Parent, and Lead. Gotham Books, 2012.

- Brown, Brené. The Power of Vulnerability. TEDxHouston, June 2010.

- Clear, James. Atomic Habits: An Easy & Proven Way to Build Good Habits & Break Bad Ones. Avery, 2018.

- Dalio, Ray. Principles: Life and Work. Simon & Schuster, 2017.

- Disney, Roy E. Quoted in Disney corporate culture materials, c. 1990s.

- Eliot, George. Middlemarch. William Blackwood and Sons, 1871–72.

- Finley, John Huston. Quoted in The New York Times, April 26, 1946.

- Frankl, Viktor E. Man's Search for Meaning. Beacon Press, 1946.

- Harrison, Scott. Thirst: A Story of Redemption, Compassion, and a Mission to Bring Clean Water to the World. Currency, 2018.

- Hardy, Darren. The Compound Effect. Vanguard Press, 2010.

- Isaacson, Walter. Steve Jobs. Simon & Schuster, 2011.

- Jung, C.G. Aion: Researches into the Phenomenology of the Self. Princeton University Press, 1951.

- Jung, C.G. Modern Man in Search of a Soul. Routledge, 1933.

- Jung, C.G. The Red Book: Liber Novus. Edited by Sonu Shamdasani. W.W. Norton & Company, 2009.

- King, Maxwell. The Good Neighbor: The Life and Work of Fred Rogers. Abrams Press, 2018.

- Maathai, Wangari. Unbowed: A Memoir. Alfred A. Knopf, 2006.

- Mann, Thomas. Reflections of a Nonpolitical Man. Secker & Warburg, 1983 [orig. 1918].

- Mann, Thomas. Death in Venice and Other Tales. Translated by Richard and Clara Winston. Vintage International, 1989.

- Murakami, Haruki. What I Talk About When I Talk About Running. Knopf, 2008.

- Mycoskie, Blake. Start Something That Matters. Spiegel & Grau, 2011.

- Newman, John Henry. Apologia Pro Vita Sua. 1864.

- Phelps, Michael, and Alan Abrahamson. No Limits: The Will to Succeed. Free Press, 2008.

- Peterson, Jordan B. Maps of Meaning: The Architecture of Belief. Routledge, 1999.

- Peterson, Jordan B. 12 Rules for Life: An Antidote to Chaos. Random House Canada, 2018.

- Rogers, Fred. The World According to Mister Rogers: Important Things to Remember. Hachette Books, 2003.

- Shaw, George Bernard. (Attributed). Maxims for Revolutionists. 1903.

- Sinek, Simon. Start with Why: How Great Leaders Inspire Everyone to Take Action. Portfolio, 2009.

- Spitz, Bob. The Beatles: The Biography. Little, Brown and Company, 2005.

- Tracy, Brian. Maximum Achievement: Strategies and Skills That Will Unlock Your Hidden Powers to Succeed. Simon & Schuster, 1993.

- Vance, Ashlee. Elon Musk: Tesla, SpaceX, and the Quest for a Fantastic Future. HarperCollins, 2015.

- Vujicic, Nick. Life Without Limits: Inspiration for a Ridiculously Good Life. WaterBrook, 2010.

- Vujicic, Nick. Unstoppable: The Incredible Power of Faith in Action. WaterBrook, 2012.

- Yousafzai, Malala, and Christina Lamb. I Am Malala: The Girl Who Stood Up for Education and Was Shot by the Taliban. Little, Brown and Company, 2013.

- Philosophy & Classics

- Aurelius, Marcus. Meditations. Translated by Gregory Hays. Modern Library, 2002.

- Diogenes Laërtius. Lives of Eminent Philosophers. c. 3rd century.

- Heraclitus. Quoted in Diogenes Laërtius, *Lives of Eminent Philosophers*, c. 3rd century.

- Lao Tzu. *Tao Te Ching*. 6th century BCE.

- Historical Figures & Speeches

- Churchill, Winston S. *Never Give In! The Best of Winston Churchill's Speeches*. Edited by Winston S. Churchill. Hyperion, 2003.

- Jobs, Steve. Commencement Address at Stanford University, June 12, 2005.

- Kennedy, John F. Address at the University of Notre Dame, May 17, 1963.

- Mandela, Nelson. *Long Walk to Freedom*. Little, Brown and Company, 1994.

Other Sources

- World Economic Forum. "Workers now have multiple careers and jobs." World Economic Forum, May 3, 2023. https://www.weforum.org/stories/2023/05/workers-multiple-careers-jobs-skills